The
Collector's
Handbook

The
Collector's
Handbook

Tax Planning, Strategy and Estate
Advice for Collectors and their Heirs.

James L. Halperin, Gregory J. Rohan
With
Mark Prendergast

Edited by
Noah Fleisher and Karl Chiao

IvyPress, Inc.

Dallas, Texas

This book is designed to provide helpful information for collectors to use in
legitimate tax planning. This information should be used in conjunction with - and
not as a substitute for - professional advice. Each taxpayer has a unique set of facts.
Every tax rule has exceptions. The law, and the interpretation of laws, may change at
any time (and they do!).

Tax laws are quite complex. Do not self-diagnose. Instead, develop a close working
relationship with a reputable tax advisor.

Check with your tax advisor before each significant transaction. Seek a second
opinion if you're still not comfortable, and ask that all advice be provided to you in
writing.

Choose the members of your financial team wisely, and don't be afraid to pay for
good advice; it will save you money in the long run. Introduce your CPA to your
attorney, financial planner, insurance agent and banker. Encourage them to work
together, since a team can accomplish much more than individuals.

Please remember that tax planning is an ongoing process - not an annual event. A
strategy that suits you well now may not meet your needs in a few months.

Collectors have special needs, and tax laws affect each one in a different way.

ISBN: 1-59967-145-X

Manufactured in the United States of America
©2011, Revised Edition

" …It is for everyone in numismatics and is even a 'must have' for those who may become heirs, but lack the know-how of what to do next. Senior citizens, like myself, will be especially happy with the interesting stories of estates, etc. … EVERYONE should own it if coins are involved in their activities. I highly recommend this book… "
– Lee Martin, Founder of the Numismatic Literary Guild

" How comprehensive is this book? I put it with my collection and told my daughter Sara to read it when it comes to handling my coin estate. "
– Fred Weinberg, Past President of the Professional Numismatists Guild

" In summary, this small paperback book, with fewer than 130 pages, contains a wealth of information for collectors at all levels of the hobby. You can read it over a weekend, and I would urge you to share it with your potential heirs. If nothing else, place a copy on top of your collection, with important (to you) sections highlighted. Your heirs will be glad you did. "
– Mike Thorne, Writer. Coins Magazine
Estate Planning Made Easy, June 3, 2009

The first edition of this book, titled
The Rare Coin Estate Book, received the comments
and endorsements listed above, and was also
Winner of the Robert Friedberg Award from the
Professional Numismatists Guild:
Best Numismatic Book of the Year
Now rewritten for all forms of art, jewelry
and collectibles!

Contents

Forward

···

WHY WE COLLECT THINGS

My friend, John Jay Pittman, did not start out a wealthy man. Instead, he resolutely assembled a vast, renowned coin collection. He accomplished this through relentless study and the shrewd investment of a significant portion of his limited income as a middle manager for Eastman Kodak, supplemented by his wife's income as a schoolteacher.

In 1954, he mortgaged the family house to travel to Egypt and bid on coins at the King Farouk Collection auction. He demanded many more sacrifices of himself and his family over the decades, all in the name of collecting. He passed away in 1996, with no apparent regrets, and his long-suffering family deservingly received the benefit of his efforts when the collection was sold at auction for more than $30 million.

The question remains: Why did he do it?

On our Website, HA.com, we auction many different types of collectibles in addition to rare coins and currency. Most of our 500,000+ registered client/bidders collect in more than one area, which we can determine through online surveys, free catalogs and multiple drawings for prizes throughout the year. Our clients seek many different collectibles, and for many different reasons.

One fervent collector of historical documents refers to his own collecting propensity as "a genetic defect." More likely it's basic human instinct; a survival advantage amplified by eons of natural selection. Those of our ancient ancestors who managed to accumulate scarce objects may have been more prone to survive long enough to bear offspring. Even today, wealth correlates to longer life expectancy — and could any form of wealth be more basic than scarce, tangible objects?

More relevant, though, than today's decision to collect Lithuanian first day covers or 1950s romance comic books are your long-term objectives to acquire them. Understanding your goals can help you achieve them.

If you collect, or ever plan to collect, your first priority should be developing honest self-awareness of your personal ambitions; predict how those ambitions are likely to evolve throughout your life.
In addition to the instinctive predilection previously discussed, the most common reasons people collect things include:

1) Knowledge and learning.
2) Relaxation and stress reduction.
3) Personal pleasure (including appreciation of beauty, and pride of ownership).
4) Social interaction with fellow collectors and others (i.e. the sharing of pleasure and knowledge).
5) Competitive challenge.
6) Recognition by fellow collectors and, perhaps, even non-collectors.
7) Altruism (since many great collections are ultimately donated to museums and learning institutions).
8) The desire to control, possess and bring order to a small (or even a massive) part of the world.
9) Nostalgia and/or a connection to history.
10) Accumulation and diversification of wealth, (which can ultimately provide a measure of security and freedom).

Like John Pittman, Robert Lesser is a true collector, but also a visionary with the ability to change his own course. He funded his subsequent collections by assembling a fine collection of Disney memorabilia before it was popular to do so, and later sold it for a seven-figure sum when the collecting world discovered both its importance and value. Long before anyone else discovered their now-obvious appeal, Lesser went on to assemble one of the preeminent collections of toy robots - museum exhibitions of his collection have attracted sell-out crowds with waiting lines stretching over city blocks - and pulp magazine cover paintings. His book on the latter is recommended reading, elegantly titled: Pulp Art.

Many non-acquisitive pastimes provide similar levels of satisfaction, knowledge and recognition, along with the other benefits of collecting. Unlike home gardeners, tropical fish enthusiasts, and similar hobbyists, serious collectors of rare objects will very often find that they have created substantial wealth at the end of the day, especially when they acknowledge, in an important moment of self-honesty and awareness, that this is one of their objectives.

Whatever your motivation is in collecting, this book will make you a more intelligent collector. Nearly every collection involves making reasonable financial decisions; doing so repeatedly will improve the monetary value that you, and your heirs, will ultimately reap from your collecting endeavors. We strongly encourage you to follow this advice during your collecting years, so that your heirs can enjoy your legacy, instead of spending their time resolving the problems improper planning left behind.

JESSIE WILLCOX SMITH (American, 1863-1935)
A Child's Garden of Verses (detail), book illustration, 1905
Sold For: $310,700 February 2010

Acknowledgements

Writing a book is like forming a great collection: many people will contribute in many different ways. While collecting, we build on the work of dealers, auction firms, friends old and new, and those dedicated authors whose reference books line our shelves. It is no different here. We offer many thanks to the following for their assistance during the preparation of this work:

Carlos Cardoza, Mary Hermann, Steve Ivy, Bob Korver, Burnett Marus, Steve Roach, Matthew S. Wilcox, Will Rossman, James Freedland, Noah Fleisher and Mark Van Winkle.

JASPER FRANCIS CROPSEY
Greenwood Lake, Autumn on the Hudson, 1875
Sold for: $215,100 November 2009

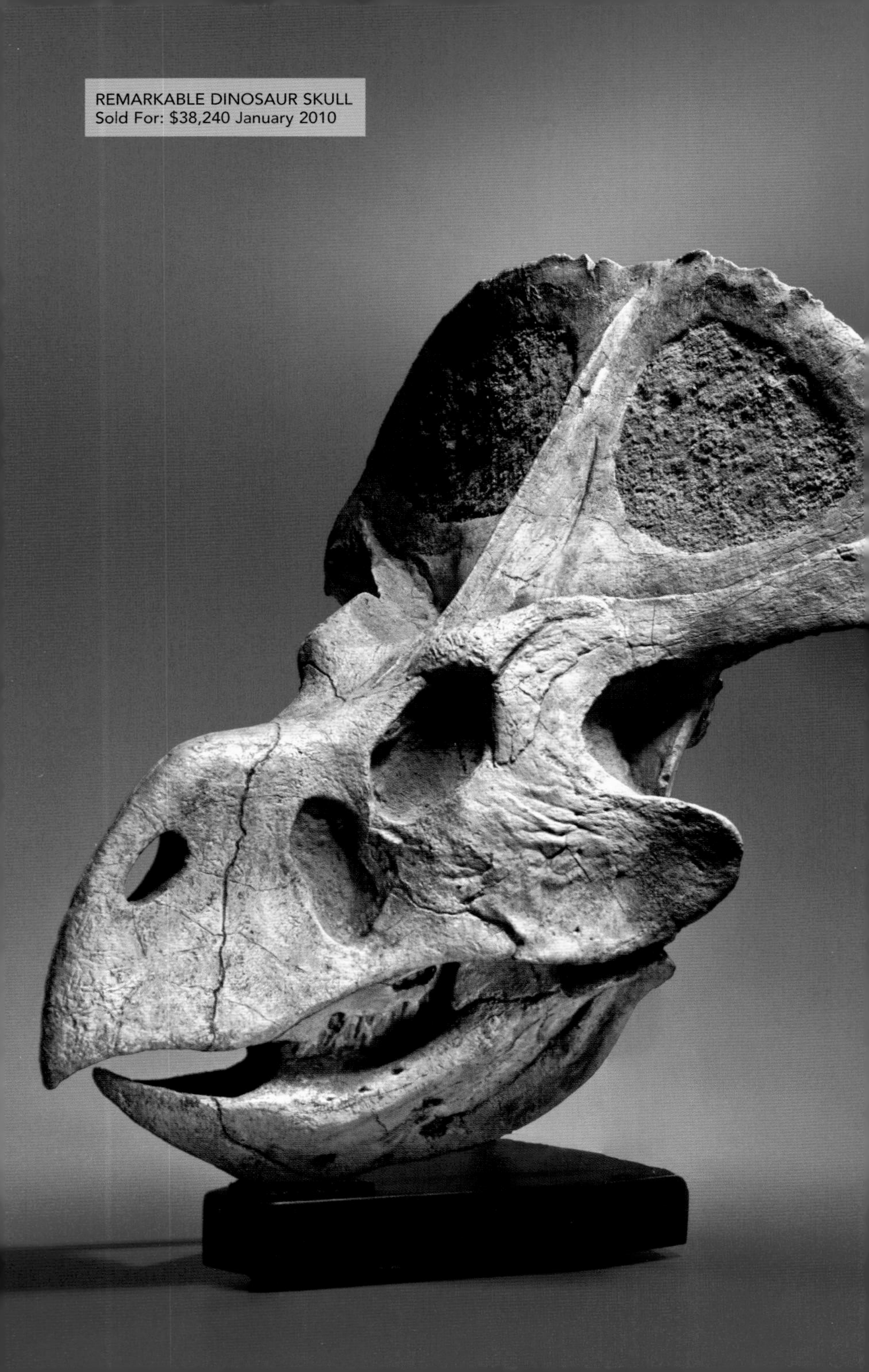

REMARKABLE DINOSAUR SKULL
Sold For: $38,240 January 2010

Introduction

We collectors know the joy that comes from surrounding ourselves with wonderful objects. The study of the pieces in our personal collections adds depth, color, and richness to our lives. We also know that a collection is intensely personal and as such, infrequently shared with others. Our history and relationships with heirs of collectors clearly indicates the problems that result from such secrecy when the collector dies.

A true collector acquires objects because they love to collect. A well-chosen collection, though, has the added benefit of appreciating in value. Many collectors, while devoting a great deal of time and energy to planning for our more traditional investments, such as stocks and bonds, neglect to do the same for our collections. You know your collection intimately. More than likely, your heirs do not.

The principals at Heritage Auctions have written this book to provide, in one place, information useful to collectors organizing their collection, advisors working with these collections, and heirs who have inherited a collection. Organizations that have received collections as donations will also benefit from this book.

To maximize the value of a collection, planning is required. That planning is minimal when compared with the care that you expended in acquiring your collection. It is with some thoughtful preparation, then, that the collection you've worked so hard to assemble can provide for those you care about; it can serve them as a blessing, not a burden.

PART ONE

Administering Your Collection

The Hon. Paul H. Buchanan, Jr. Collection
HENRY FRANÇOIS FARNY (American, 1847-1916)
Saddling Up (detail), 1895
Sold For: $334,600 June 2009

. . . .

Record Keeping

We once appraised a home with no fewer than six Federal mahogany chests of drawers. The decedent's will stated that a particular heir should receive "the good one." While the collector certainly understood which of the six was "the good one," the executor and attorney did not. Nor did the appraised values necessarily correspond with the collector's intent.

In another situation, concerning a room full of paintings, the will provided specific instructions for a specific painting, "the one with the banana." The heirs, executor and attorney all looked imploringly to us to determine which painting represented a banana. Alas, it was impossible to find any resemblance in the group, since all of the art pieces were entirely abstract. Both of these incidents, although unusual, are true.

These issues could have been completely avoided if the collections had simply been inventoried and numbered. Even where the terms of the will designate the exact location of an item in an effort to distinguish it from similar ones, it may not entirely resolve the problem. Location fields must be accurate to be diagnostic. As collectors relocate, downsize, or simply re-arrange their homes, the location of an item may change. Its unique ID number does not.

Documenting what you own by writing it down is simply the most fundamental part of intelligent collections management. For historians and scholars, original hand-written inventories have proved most valuable tools, whether in accurately renovating a historic building, understanding a major battle, or reconstructing a seminal art collection that has been dispersed. The oldest known examples of writing in Europe are lists of commodities found in the storerooms of palaces of Bronze Age Greece. Today, with computers, the process is easier than ever, and collectors of all types should understand the valuable benefits of maintaining a proper documentation standard.

Whether physically managing your collections, tracking profit and loss, or working with insurers, dealers or auction houses, a complete, documented written reference will soon become the "good book" of your collection. As an estate appraiser, the unfortunate results of poor collection inventory control are quite apparent and disconcerting. Nobody understands your collections as well as you do, making you the most qualified person to document them in a proper inventory. Inputting and documenting each new acquisition as you proceed will make this process manageable and prove most helpful as your collection grows.

Handwritten or Computer Generated: The choice is yours to document your collection these days, you might use a simple Excel spreadsheet, a Quicken list, a personal Website, hand-written note cards, the My Collection feature on the Heritage Website, or even some private software options like Collectify. While any method is better than no method, one should keep in mind that a good inventory system must not only make sense to the collector, it must - as we cannot point out enough - make sense to those who might need to use it in the future: children, executors and attorneys – all of whom may have little understanding about the property in your collection. Highly specialized jargon, abbreviations and personal notation codes should be avoided, while certain clear fields of information, and a consistent format, become key features of a written inventory.

Different types of collectible property will require different information fields, but a general checklist may run as follows:

Coin Inventory

For coin and comic collectors, HA.com has a free and particularly useful feature called "My Collection" which allows the collector to keep a private record of items owned, bought, or sold.

Object type: What is it?

Title: Is the object well known? e.g. the "Mona Lisa"

Maker: Is the creator known?

Medium: What's it made of?

Size: Dimensions and/or weight

Inscriptions: Is anything written on it?

Signature: Did the maker sign it?

Subject: Is there a representation on the item?

Date: When was it made?

Manner of Acquisition: How did you obtain it? Auction, yard sale, etc.

Cost/Date: What and when did you pay for it?

Location: Where is the item? A safety deposit box, den, on loan to local museum?

Provenance: Ownership history of the item, if known

Special Notes: Any relevant information about the object.

Photographs: Take a picture of each item in your collection.

File Folder: Keep or scan copies of all relevant documentation - invoices, auction catalog entries, bills of lading, etc.

The Art of Inventory Control: Tying it all Together

Even the most accurate inventory documentation will lose its utility if it is not "tied" to the actual objects. Tying data to an object involves giving each item a unique inventory number – with which it is tagged or marked, and which cross-references the written inventory entry and a photograph.

A useful collection inventory number system should begin with the year of acquisition, followed by an individual item number, such as 2007.001.

It is critical that the object, photograph, number tag, and master inventory do not become separated. The best solution is to attach an object's unique inventory number to the object itself, if possible. String tags and sticker labels are often used, when safe to apply, but can be removed easily. One superior museum method for marrying an ID number to its object in a safe and reversible way (on some types of objects) is to find a part of the piece not seen or decorated

An American Renaissance Revival Style Cabinet
Sold For: $71,700 October 2006

– usually the bottom or back - and put a small strip of varnish down.
After it dries, the ID number is written in ink, and when that dries,
another coat of varnish is placed over the number. For paintings,
one should mark only the back stretchers or frames with the work's
unique ID number. Each type of property presents its own numbering
challenges. The application of the ID number must not harm or
compromise the object's aesthetic qualities. Often, the only solution
is to tag the box or plastic sleeve in which an object is stored.

Today, bar code technology, microchips and even radioactive
isotope staining have enhanced our tagging options. Do your

research to see what's out there and what's best for your particular collection. The best way to tag a coin, for instance, may not be the best way to tag a comic book, or a piece of fine art.

When photographing an object, write its unique ID number on a piece of paper and place it in the picture field so that the photograph actually shows the object and the number. That way, any loose photograph can be easily identified.

You'll thank yourself in the long run, as will everyone involved

We've established that the reason for documenting and numbering your collection is to safeguard knowledge. Most large collections contain near-identical or duplicate items, which - to the untrained eye - may appear indistinguishable from one another, even though their subtle differences may be significant. Your appraiser, insurance company, fellow collectors and heirs will all benefit from diligent record-keeping. Daunting shelves full of antique glass paperweights, libraries of collectible comic books or cases of mechanical banks require order – whether they are to be enjoyed, gifted, or sold. It all begins with knowing what you own through the use of a detailed and updated inventory.

Finally, maintain a second copy of your complete inventory, with photographs, in a different location from the collection itself. Safety deposit boxes in banks are recommended, or even better, an electronic copy stored on a back-up disc and/or online.

When you sell or otherwise remove an item from your collection, make certain that it is noted clearly in your inventory.

Detective Comics #27 (DC, 1939)
Sold For: $1,075,500 February 2010

2

Caring For Your Collection

"He that thinks he can afford to be negligent is not far from being poor." - Samuel Johnson

"Never neglect details." - Colin Powell

After being created, all objects age; they act and react over time in accordance with their physical and chemical properties to the environment in which they exist. Metals mineralize naturally. Paper collectibles are photo-chemically changed when exposed to the light necessary for us to enjoy them. Soft fabrics become brittle, hard substances become pliable. While some changes may take centuries, others take only minutes, and the goal of the collector, like that of the museum conservator, should be to prolong life, minimize damage and minimize the aging process for our fine art and collectibles. In this manner quality and value can be safeguarded.

Human contact is frequently the leading culprit of wear and deterioration. Use of an object, whether it is a circulated coin or toy train, simply removes the pristine quality all collectibles originate with. For many items that use lessens value, but in others it raises it. A baseball glove worn out by 10 years of continued use by Ted Williams enhances its value as a result of its history, regardless of the physical condition that results from aging. Each category of collectible has its own standards governing the effect of original use on value. Once an object has left its original environment, however, and becomes a cultural collectible, the new owners must endeavor to safeguard the existing condition of the item as it is was when they received it.

Human manipulation harms objects physically and chemically through the acids in the perspiration on our hands. After that, sunlight and moisture are the two greatest detriments to most collections. Another serious threat is contact with reactive materials, such as a cleansing or sealing agent.

Human Contact
Avoiding direct contact with objects, if possible, is best.

- Coins can be placed in sealed inert capsules, which protect them from both physical and chemical harm. If outside a capsule, a coin should only be grasped by its edge, avoiding contact with its two sides.
- Paintings should be framed, and prints glazed then framed. Grasp only the frames when examining.
- Comics should be placed in Mylar sleeves, or encapsulated by CGC.
- White cotton gloves should be worn when handling anything directly. When examining a valuable ceramic lidded jar, place one hand on the lid and the other under the base, so that the lid does not fall off while being moved. Statues in any medium should never be grasped by their extending parts, e.g. the arms and legs of figural works.
- The shape, medium and condition of each piece determine its unique handling criteria.

Sunlight and Artificial Light
If you have ever noticed a rich dark mahogany table bleached off-white and cracked due to its location near a window, you have witnessed the powerful effect of light on objects. Prolonged exposure to ultraviolet light may destroy valuable furniture, paintings, photographs, books and textiles.

If you wish to keep your collections in plain view, certain steps should be taken to minimize light damage:

- Purchase windows that filter UV light.
- Place UV filter sleeves over fluorescent lighting.
- Glaze framed items with UV filtering acrylic, not glass (not appropriate for all media).
- Curtains and blinds should be hung to filter sunlight.

Circa 1940 Babe Ruth Single
Signed Baseball
Sold For: $20,315 April 2010

- Never locate a light-sensitive object in direct sunlight.
- Keep sensitive works covered with protective cloth; remove only when viewing.

Water and Moisture

Most water damage is caused not by rain, burst pipes or floods (although all are relevant and hazardous), but by water vapor; simple humidity in the air that surrounds an object. Organic materials deteriorate in a high relative humidity (RH); mold and mildew can grow, and metals mineralize at a greater rate.

The specific recommended RH for your types of collectibles should be determined and the appropriate steps taken to protect it from air conditioning, humidifying or dehumidifying. It is important to avoid large fluctuations in RH and temperature, as these fluctuations may cause serious stress to any object.

1907 Ultra High Relief, $20 Lettered
Edge PR69 PCGS
Sold For: $2,990,000 November 2005

Reactive Materials

It is not unusual to find 19th century prints on pulp paper in their original frames, with acid-rich mats, fixed with glued tape, backed by thin planks of pine and secured with iron-alloy nails. We have since learned a great deal about reactive chemistry and understand that the old practices are a recipe for disaster.

The acid in the mat will leech out to the print, causing discoloration or mat burn. Other acids in the adhesive tape will do likewise. The wood backer and frame, designed to protect the print, are full of acetic acid, formic acid, formaldehyde and other chemicals which can damage or destroy the artwork. Finally, the iron nails reacting to the wood and moist air will corrode quickly, harming anything in close proximity.

Today, even our urban, industrialized air contains sulfur dioxide and nitrogen dioxide which can create an acidic environment in the presence of elevated relative humidity.

It is imperative that collectors learn what conditions will affect their particular collections. Outdoor marble statuary will not be harmed greatly by sunlight or termites, but acid rain will quickly do the job unless a protective wax is applied routinely. Each type of art, antique and collectible has its own preservation requirements.

Educate Yourself

Art and collectibles usually trade in a commercial context, so don't assume the frames, wrappers, backboards, plastic sleeves or other materials that may house your artworks or collectibles at the time of purchase are the safest ones available for the continued health of your acquisitions. It is more likely that these materials were the most affordable option for your dealer, auctioneer or private seller.

Caring for your collection properly requires learning the safest and most updated methods available for viewing, displaying and storing items. Each object will have unique issues relevant to its own material, form and condition.

Museum and conservation information is readily available in books and online. A good reference is: Conservation Concerns: A Guide for Collectors and Curators. Konstanze Bachman (Ed.).

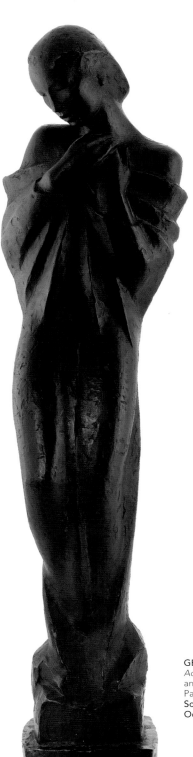

GEORG KOLBE
Adagio, conceived in 1923
and cast in the late 1920's
Patinated bronze
Sold for: $86,637
October 2009

3

Safeguarding Your Collection

The unfortunate truth is that crimes against property are on the rise. Burglary and theft almost qualify as growth businesses. The current arrest and conviction rate is abysmal, and restoration of property even worse. It has even come to pass in recent years that some of our own employees have fallen victim to airport "snatch and grab" thefts.

The good news was that the thieves thought that they seized a box of coins, when all they actually took was a box of coin supplies. The bad news was that despite being provided descriptions of both of the perpetrators and a license plate number, the police were not optimistic - or perhaps not interested - in pursuing the matter further. The fact that the thieves absconded with the wrong bags made the case relatively "insignificant" in the overall scope of things. We don't know if that type of attitude is endemic; perhaps there are only enough personnel resources to react to the more serious crimes these days. In any event, it certainly illustrates the need for each of us to become more vigilant concerning security, particularly if we own the kind of valuables sought after by thieves.

SECURITY VERSUS ACCESS — A TIMELESS QUANDARY

Most collectors prefer their collectibles be close at hand to study and enjoy at their leisure, which is what collecting is all about. Routinely transporting the collection to and from a safe-deposit box is tiresome at best. Conversely, no one wants to lose their favorite collectibles to a burglar. The unfortunate fact is that the inconvenience is constant and the significance of security is apparent only after you've been robbed. As a result, even people who know better may become lax over time. To avoid this, write your own personal security plan and include these elements:

HOME SECURITY – your collection is at risk from theft, fire, water damage and other natural disasters. If you are going to maintain articles of substantial value at your residence, you should consider several proactive measures to protect them:

• Monitored Security System
A security system is the core of any security plan. This includes both theft and fire alarms that are monitored externally and reported immediately and directly to police and fire departments when triggered. Hardware can be installed for a few hundred to a few thousand dollars and monitoring involves only a nominal monthly expense, currently around $25-$75. A monitored security system sends most burglars looking for easier game and puts the more daring ones on the clock. Once the system perimeter is breached, the burglar has only the response time to grab what he can and attempt an escape.

The following devices and practices are designed to minimize the number of valuables a burglar can locate quickly:

– Home Safe
Safes are obvious deterrents against theft, but have additional value in the event of fire or natural disaster. Costs are based on size and fire (temperature) "TL" rating. You should make your determination only after discussing your particular needs with an expert. Many insurance companies require a home safe to write a collectibles rider to your Homeowner's Policy, while others will discount the rider based on the quantity and quality of the safeguards you employ.

– Deterrent Practices
Whether or not you employ a security system or a safe, there are actions that will reduce the risk of a successful burglary. A primary deterrent is to always leave the impression that someone is at home. This can be accomplished in part by remembering to have your paper and mail held while you

are out of town and by placing one or more of your lights on timers. "Beware of Dog" signs (whether or not you own one) on the back fence may also be helpful in warding off a potential burglar.

– Camouflaging Valuables
Most people are predictable, and burglars know all the "good" hiding places. They still must act within external or self-imposed time constraints. The longer a burglar remains in a house, the greater the likelihood of capture; a burglar understands that as well. Things you should know and avoid: most people keep their valuables in the master bedroom followed closely by their home offices, if they have one. Guess where burglars go first? So, leave decoys.
One gentleman we know has numerous coin albums (filled with pocket change) in plain sight on the bookshelves. Another acquaintance has an old safe that is heavy but moveable. It resides in the corner of his home office and contains absolutely nothing. Its predecessor was removed in a burglary where the thief left several thousand dollars worth of electronic and musical equipment because he thought that he hit the jackpot.
The acquaintance now has a monitored security system and modern (wall) safe, but keeps the decoy as a reminder of the importance of security, and perhaps just a bit of humor about the burglar who was the recipient of naught save an empty box (and maybe a hernia). If you don't own a safe, small valuables are best hidden in a false outlet with an object plugged into it. A collection of small items should be spread over several non-obvious locations. While you may not be able to totally foil a burglar, you may at least be able to minimize his success.

• Off-Site Storage & Transport
The primary off-site storage option is a safe-deposit box at either a bank or private vault. If you can find a location close to home or work, the inconvenience factor can be minimized. Sites with weekend

access are a major advantage, if scarce. There is no question that safe-deposit boxes offer very secure storage, but do not allow that to lull you into complacency. There are still a few storage and security guidelines you need to remember and follow:

- Rent a box that is large enough to hold everything easily.
- Use a desiccant such as silica gel to remove any moisture, and change it regularly.
- Never forget that your greatest security danger is in transporting the collectibles to and from the box. Use a nondescript bag or carry-all to hold them, and try not to carry too much weight at one time.
- Have someone drive you to the box site or park as close to the entrance as possible to minimize your time on the street with the valuables.
- Avoid establishing a pattern in picking up or dropping off your collection.
- Be aware of your surroundings when transporting your collectibles. Check your rearview mirror frequently. If you believe that a vehicle may be following you, do not drive directly to your home. Make several detours that do not follow any logical traffic pattern and see if you are able to lose the suspect vehicle. Know where the closest police station is relative to the storage facility and if you become firmly convinced that you are being followed, drive directly there.
- Carry a cell phone with you when transporting valuables. A frightening new robbery technique is to rear-end a vehicle and then rob the victim when he or she exits to assess the damage and exchange insurance information. You will have to use your judgment in this situation, but if you are carrying valuables and are rear-ended, you should remain in the car and call 911. Don't hesitate to tell the operator that you are carrying valuables and are concerned about the possibility of robbery. If you really believe that it is a setup, don't stop; call 911 and explain to them the situation while driving to the police station.

– Airports have also become a favorite hub for thieves. There is a steady flow of people, noise, confusion and a sense of urgency from people trying to meet deadlines in an unfamiliar environment. The usual method is the snatch and grab, as we mentioned above; the thief targets someone who appears distracted, grabs their briefcase or bag and melts into the crowd.

A variation on this theme is when teams of operatives are located where baggage is being unloaded at the curb. One or more of the thieves will distract the victim, while others will grab the bags, then all of them will make their escape in a waiting vehicle. Your only protection is constant vigilance. You should always either have a grip

From a New Jersey Estate
R. LALIQUE
Rare perfume bottle for 'Raquel Meller' fragrance by Roditi & Sons, enameled on each face in orange and black, circa 1925
Sold For: $20,315 December 2010

or your foot on any case containing valuables and should become deeply suspicious if a stranger tries to engage you in conversation.

Strange as it sounds, some people carry a loud whistle when transporting valuables. If someone attempts to grab a bag and you start blowing the whistle, the thief is put on the defensive. Everyone else in the area is confused or startled by the noise and the thief loses the camouflage of the crowd.

• Shipping

Occasionally, you may need to ship valuable articles to another party. Again, there are rules that you can follow to minimize the possibility of loss. First and foremost, do not attach anything on the outside of the package that would hint at its contents. If an address contains identifying words—coins, numismatics, gold, antiques, or anything similar—use initials instead. Additionally, look at the container you're using. We recently received a package from another dealer whose mailing address labels used initials, but the shipping person packed the coins in a "Redbook" box that was clearly marked, "Guidebook of U.S. Coins."

Pack the items securely so that they do not rattle and betray their presence. Loose spaces (such as in tubes) should be filled. Pieces of Styrofoam "peanuts" are good for this purpose. Make sure that your shipping box is strong enough for the included weight and bind it with strapping tape. If you are using Registered Mail (the preferred method for most collectors), the post office has a requirement that all access seams be sealed with an approved paper tape.

Method of shipment involves a decision that weighs value, risk and cost. USPS 1st Class or Priority Mail with Insurance is the most cost-effective method up to $500 in value. The rate of loss has dropped considerably over the last decade, so this is a reasonable option for inexpensive items that can be replaced. Above the $500 value, Registered Mail with Postal Insurance is both cost-effective and extremely safe. The one caveat is that the real insurance maximum for registered mail is $25,000. The Post Office requires you to indicate if the contents exceed that amount, and will charge you more for a higher claimed value; they will not, however, pay more than $25,000 on a claim. If the value exceeds that amount, you will need to send multiple packages or obtain supplemental private insurance.

Fed-Ex, UPS and other private shippers have become popular in recent years. They offer fast, guaranteed delivery with a high success rate. They also offer some insurance options, but rare coins are specifically excluded. You will need to obtain private insurance coverage if you use one of these shippers, or you may request that the other party insure the shipment if they have sufficient coverage available and a shipper account.

• Insurance

No matter how many security measures you employ to protect your collection, you will also need to acquire suitable insurance to protect yourself should you suffer a loss of part or all of the collection. This can be a complicated area, as insurance companies write policies in a language all their own. This is not offered as a criticism of insurance companies, who we understand are in business to make money and also perform a valuable service.

As someone seeking protection, though, you need to understand that contract language will generally favor the insurance company, and you need to know exactly what coverage you are, or are not, receiving. That means asking questions. In the case of coins, you need to be particularly certain of what coverage applies when the coins are at home, in a safe-deposit box or in transit, as well as any additional security requirements for each circumstance. It is not a cut-and-dry situation.

For example:

Most Home Owner's policies DO NOT insure your coin or jewelry collection beyond $1,000 (combined with all other items defined as a "valuable"). Your insurance company will usually offer you a rider for more specific coverage, but as it's not their standard business, they are typically not very flexible. You will be required to provide a fixed inventory and it would likely be a major paperwork exercise to modify the coverage whenever you buy or sell items from your collection.

Some insurance companies may require an "appraisal for insurance." If you choose a company that has this requirement, guidance is available in Chapter Nine.

As in most business circumstances, you should analyze your options against your personal situation and then find the best result for you. In this specialized field, the best option often comes from a company that is familiar with the needs of collectors. If this route appeals to you, we have listed several companies in the Appendix to this book titled, "Insurance Companies Offering Collectible and Numismatic Coverage."

In the case of collectibles other than coins, you may want to ask a dealer to recommend a knowledgeable insurance company. Not all insurance companies possess the expertise or the appropriate coverage that is involved with collectibles. Price is not the only consideration. Premiums may vary, however. Some insurance companies have a reputation for not acting in a timely manner when coverage is an issue. They may be slow or reluctant in responding to the situation and slow in paying the claim. They may also dispute the amount of the loss. Find an agent and a company with a good reputation and expertise in the field of collectibles. You may have to pay a little more, but it will be well worth the price if you ever have to submit a significant claim.

Coins and other small items are popular with burglars and thieves. Regretfully, the risk involved means you need to temper your enjoyment of collecting with some caution. In addition to the measures already suggested, you need to be careful about discussing your collection (and where you keep it) with others. It is believed that any information shared with one person reaches 10, and an interesting piece of information… well, use your imagination. Enjoy your collection, but stay vigilant.

TIPS FOR HEIRS: This chapter contains advice that may be the most important you will read. Seasoned collectors are generally very security conscious, but those who come into possession of a collection only recently must immediately understand the risks and responsibilities that come with this unfamiliar asset. Most urgent of all, take the collection (if it's small enough) to a safe deposit box immediately. Until you have it safely transferred into a bank vault, do not discuss it with others. With larger objects, you may want to consult with an insurance agent about the best method to safeguard them until they can be dispersed.

ANDY WARHOL
Cowboys and Indians
(set of 10), 1986
Sold For: $149,375
October 2010

PART TWO

Estate Planning for your Collection

Cartier Magnificent & Rare Diamond,
Jade, Pearl, Coral & Rock Crystal
Mystery Clock, No. 202085
Sold For: $155,350 December 2009

4

Include Your Family In Your Plans

Hardly any adult in America has not read, or at least heard about the importance of making a will or a trust. Yet every year, tens of thousands of Americans whose family would have benefited from a will die without one. The reason is simple: nobody likes to think about death, much less actively prepare for it. It may be even worse for collectors.

As much as people avoid contemplating their own demise, collectors are equally reluctant to consider the sale of their collectibles. Perhaps they equate the two events. Dying is not a pleasant subject. The great wit and philosopher, Woody Allen, may have stated it best when confronted with a life threatening operation. He told his physician, "Doctor, I'm not afraid of dying, I just don't want to be there when it happens."

Another well known quotation from Benjamin Franklin is worth restating, "Certainly, in the world nothing is certain but death and taxes," and we are sure about the latter (taxes) and maybe not that certain about the former (death).

Since you have already made the decision to read this book, we hope that you are at least willing to consider the ultimate disposition of your acquisitions. Whether you intend to collect to the end of your life, or sell next month, much of the same advice applies. Heritage Auctions has assisted thousands of people in disposing of their collections, and more than 20% were heirs who possessed little knowledge regarding the collectibles. That is one statistic that we would like to change. You should too.

Involve Your Family

Many collectors keep their families in the dark as to the scale and nature of their collecting. We understand that the reasons for this may be myriad and that they may very well suit your current situation and preference. Taking a longer view, however, have you considered the effect that an untimely demise might have on your collection? What would your heirs' expectations be? What should be done with it? Should it be sold? Distributed among family members? Or both? What will remain after taxes? We have seen all extremes.

One call from Widow Smith (not her real name, of course) brought us to a house where we found a dining room table covered with boxes of world coins to a height of three feet. From a distance, it was one of the most impressive collections that we had ever inspected: all matching coin boxes, all neatly labeled with the countries of origin. The widow told us that her husband had been a serious collector for more than three decades, visiting his local coin shop nearly every Saturday. He then came home and meticulously prepared his purchases, spending hour upon happy hour at the table in his little study.

We opened the first box, and couldn't help but notice the neat and orderly presentation: cardboard 2x2s, neatly stapled, crisp printing of country name, year of issue, Yeoman number, date purchased, and amount paid. We also couldn't help but notice that 90% of the coins had been purchased for less than 50 cents and the balance for less than one dollar each. The collection contained box after box of post-1940 minors, all impeccably presented. All essentially worthless.

We asked Mrs. Smith if she had any idea of the value of the collection. She replied that she knew that rare coins were valuable, and since her late husband had worked so diligently on his collection for so many years, she assumed that the proceeds would enable her to afford a nice retirement in Florida. It was obviously a very delicate moment.

We had to carefully explain that we were neither interested in the coins for auction, nor for direct purchase. Her husband had enjoyed himself thoroughly for all those years, but he had never told her that he was spending more on holders, staples and boxes than he was on the coins. Her dreams of comfortable retirement diminished, we advised her to contact two dealers who routinely purchase such coins (She refused to consider an offer from the local dealer who had sold most of these coins to her husband). Mr. Smith's fault was not in his collecting, for his love of these coins was manifest, but in his failure to inform his wife as to what he was doing.

We more typically encounter widows and heirs on the other extreme. When your spouse spends $50,000 or $100,000 on rare coins or other collectibles, you generally have some knowledge of those purchases, but not always, and not always to the full extent of the purchases. Rare collectibles at this level are definitely an asset that needs to be given appropriate consideration. Unfortunately, because collectibles are a hard asset, one that easily falls outside of prying eyes, some heirs designate their distributions without first gathering all of the facts.

Miss Jones was the younger of two sisters who were dividing their father's estate. Dad had left Germany in the early 1930s. As historians will note, this was not particularly a great time to immigrate to America, although it was certainly an excellent time to be leaving Germany. Dad brought to America two collections: antique silver service pieces and his rare coins. The coins were mostly sold to establish his mercantile concern in Iowa. He prospered despite the hard times, and he devoted the next thirty years to rebuilding his collection of Germanic/European coinage.

At the same time, he continued to expand his collection of silverware lovingly created by 17th and 18th century German silversmiths. We knew every aspect of his collecting history, because he left a meticulous record on index cards. Every coin, every piece of silver was detailed with his cataloging and purchase history. Even his own daughter was moved to compliment his passion for maintaining such detailed records.

After his death, his daughters decided to split his collections between themselves. They added up the purchase values of each of his collections, which were just about equal; something we do not believe was coincidental. The older sister/executor had acquired some small knowledge of antique silver, and since she wished to keep all of the elegant heirloom tea service for herself, she decided to keep the silver and give her younger sister the coins. She was definitely not interested in splitting. She sold the non-family silver pieces through a regional auction house, and boasted of realizing more than $200,000 from her father's $27,000 investment.

A Pair of George III Silver Candelabra
Sold For: $53,775 April 2007

The younger sister came to us with only one box of his coins. Her father's records for that box indicated a cost less than $2,000, but knowing the years he had collected, we were anticipating at least a few nice coins. However, we were totally unprepared for the numismatic feast which was laid before us: pristine coins of the greatest rarity—wonderful, gorgeous coins, most of which had been removed from the market for at least twenty years. His "$2,000" box was worth more than $150,000, surpassing her wildest expectations.

Miss Jones then produced the record cards for the rest of the collection, and we offered to travel back to Iowa with her the same day. When we finished auctioning the coins, she had realized more than $1.2 million. Here's one more example of what can occur when information is not shared. Be warned: the ending is a shocker.

The wife of a deceased coin dealer once called us to consign $1 million dollars in rare coins from her late husband's estate. Since her self-employed husband had been ill for some time, this asset represented a significant portion of all of her retirement assets. We eagerly picked up the coins, and had already started cataloging and photographing when we received an urgent phone call from her attorney. The coins had to be returned immediately. It appeared that her husband had been holding the extensive coin purchases of his main customer in his vaults, and he had neither informed his wife nor adequately marked the boxes. Most of her $1 million retirement asset belonged to her husband's client and not to her husband. Failure to adequately inform heirs doesn't happen just to collectors.

A final example that really distressed us demonstrates that partial planning, no matter how well intentioned, cannot always guarantee the desired outcome. A collector with sizeable holdings divided his coins equally (by value) between his adult son and daughter, with instructions that they should seek expert advice before selling. The daughter came to us, and we were pleased to report that her father had done an excellent job of dividing the collection – as expertly as we could have advised. The daughter's coins were worth in excess of $85,000.

After she signed the Consignment Agreement, she told us the rest of the story. Her brother had "sold" his share eight months earlier to a local pawnbroker for less than $7,500. Her father hadn't shared his knowledge of the asset's value with his children for fear that his son would spend the money foolishly. Instead, her brother basically gave it away.

So, what should you do to prevent such problems?

Get Your Family Involved — One Way or Another

One of the greatest joys of collecting involves not just the objects of interest, but the friends we make along the way. If transferring your collection to the next generation is desirable, you will want to provide for an orderly transition. If they aren't interested in sharing your love of the collectibles, you will have to decide whether to dispose of the collection in your lifetime, or leave that decision to your heirs. If the latter, your family should – at a minimum – have a basic understanding of your collection, its approximate value, and how you want it dispersed.

Fantastic Model 1883 Gatling Gun
Sold for: $334,600 November 2007

Important Questions to Be Discussed

- Are there heirs who will want the collection from a collector's standpoint?
- Where are the objects kept?
- Where is the inventory of the collectibles kept?
- What is the approximate value of the collection?
- Has the collection been appraised or insured? If, so, where is that appraisal and does it need to be updated?
- Do any of the articles in your possession belong to someone else?

– Is there a dealer or other experts that you trust to provide guidance to your heirs?

– Is there a firm that you and your heirs will wish to use to aid in the collection's disposition after your death?

In summary, talk with your family about your collection.

The horror stories that begin this chapter are all true, none are isolated cases, and they won't be the last. If, for whatever reason, you cannot allow yourself to share this information with your whole family, choose one trusted individual — perhaps the person you are considering to be the Executor or Trustee of your estate. If that doesn't satisfy you, please take the time to write detailed instructions, or simply make notes in this book, and leave it in your safe-deposit box, or wherever you keep your valuables.

The next few chapters will further define your options and aid you in finding assistance in implementing those options. Whatever your choices, the written instructions can be incorporated in your will or trust. At minimum, you will have a document kept with your collection inventory. Your heirs will thank you for this final attention to detail.

TIPS FOR HEIRS: This chapter does not address inheritance issues, but communications can be initiated from any direction. Do you have a parent with a collection? Certainly it is an issue that requires tact, but such a discussion may save considerable heartache and misfortune later. Additionally, if you know in advance that your spouse or relative has named you as Executor in a will or the Trustee of your Trust, a few conversations about the collection will make your life much easier.

5

Division of Assets

"There is a strange charm in the thoughts of a good legacy, or the hopes of an estate, which wondrously removes or at least alleviates the sorrow that men would otherwise feel for the death of friends." -Miguel De Cervantes

Inheritances bring out the best in some families and the worst in others. It is an unfortunate fact that within even the most stable families, some members will view their relative worth only in tangible terms.

In the highly charged emotional environment surrounding the loss of a loved one, any weaknesses in the relationships of those left behind are exacerbated when a loved one has departed. Suspicious minds are more finely honed and if the estate remains for the survivors to divide, it won't take much of a spark to ignite a small conflagration. You can minimize the likelihood of a family meltdown by seeking sound legal advice (advisory team) in preparing your will or trust(s) and by leaving precise, written instructions dividing your assets among your heirs. If the collection is of substantial value, you will need to obtain legal advice from those having expertise in tax and estate planning, as well as advisors who are familiar with your particular collectibles. An insurance advisor should always be part of your advisory team, as we will discuss later.

Instructions in regard to collections are particularly important because they generally involve a large number of pieces with valuations that are not obvious based on appearance alone. This can lead to conflict. For instance, in the world of coins and currency, there are a number of varieties and variations of the same coin and date. This is where grading and authentication will pay for itself. Canadian coins have dots, maple leafs, shoulder straps and other varieties that are determinative of their value. Without the help of an expert, it is not difficult to make an expensive error.

The simplest option (administratively) is to leave the collection intact to one heir. The collection should be appraised and, if necessary, submitted to the appropriate grading or authentication service as recommended in the eighth chapter of this book, "Third Party Authentication and Grading of coins," which will establish an equitable basis for dividing the balance of your estate.

If your estate contains more than one collection (and an equal or structured division is part of your plan) you should have the other collections appraised as well to determine parity. An attorney with expertise in tax and estate planning can provide the appropriate language for your will or trust. This is considered to be the simplest option, because it stifles any disputes before they can arise surrounding the physical division of the collection after your death.

If you divide one collection among your various heirs, the paperwork burden increases. You must then designate which specific items are to be bequested to which recipient, then expand the scope of the appraisal, and more precisely, define and specify the location of each recipient's inheritance. Alternatively, you may decree "equal shares." This will also require a detailed and comprehensive appraisal, but may cause problems if two heirs want the same exact items, or if some heirs want to keep certain articles and others want to sell. You should objectively analyze your family dynamics and the financial condition of each family member in making this decision, along with any special needs that are involved as to those who are unable either mentally or emotionally to act in their own best interests.

We frequently hear the lament that there is no member in the family who enjoys or understands collectibles. We like to think that no one enjoys or understands them *yet*. It may be that many individuals devote their leisure time and have the funds to pursue their hobbies later in life and begin collecting after their children have grown up. We know how difficult it is to budget for collectibles when there are dentist and doctor bills, clothing, food and tuition to pay. By the time the children are grown, most of them have developed their own hobbies and interests. Be that as it may, we doubt that you would want your family to suffer financially over their choice of leisure activities. A simpler alternative is to establish a will or trust directing that the articles be sold, with the proceeds shared equally among the heirs rather than enduring the cumbersome process of equitably dividing a collection.

The question then arises as to whether the collection should be disposed of in your lifetime. From our experience with thousands of these situations, we can attest that it is easier to divide the proceeds of a sale than the collectibles themselves. The reasons are quite logical. Members of your family may vicariously appreciate the pleasure that your collection brought to you, but unless they are collectors themselves, they are unlikely to keep your collectibles. If you can accept that, ask yourself whether they would handle the disposition as carefully and knowledgeably as you would? If this represents a significant asset to them, are they prepared to manage it properly? As mentioned in the exemplary story in the previous chapter – dividing a collection may not equate to the same monetary distribution that you intend. Given changing markets and prices achieved through auction or private sale, a collection distribution based on perceived or appraised values may not correlate to the actual values once sold.

Also note that the values of items in a collection should not be based on insurance appraisals. These appraisals usually represent a "retail replacement" valuation which can be far different from the "fair market" valuation that would be used for financial planning or estate tax purposes and represent value closer to what could be raised by the sale of the items. Auction houses are a good source for helping determine the realistic estimate of what an item would sell for in the open market. Most provide auction estimates free of charge.

There are also a number of tax issues that must be considered, which will be discussed later. However, there are different tax consequences related to gifting assets during your lifetime and disposing of them at the time of your death. Taxation of lifetime gifts, compared to those made at death, have very different results that may influence your decision as to how to distribute or dispose of your collection. However, taxes should only be a part of your determination - not the sole consideration. As many investors fear taking profits on their equities, because there may be a tax liability, and hold on until the gain disappears, you must weigh many factors in deciding what is the best result for you, and your family, regarding your collection.

We understand if you are unable to part with your treasures, particularly if developing your collection is a major activity and source of enjoyment in your life at the present time. If this is the situation, we strongly recommend that you prepare a written disposition plan for your heirs and maintain it with your inventory. Whether you intend to collect for three years, seven or a lifetime, you need to prepare now as if you will not be available to provide guidance in the future. These are hard words, but we doubt any person has the desire to have their family suffer a financial loss through the combination of poor planning and an untimely demise or incapacitation.

The upside of choosing disposition in your lifetime is that you retain control of the process and possibly garner some recognition of your collecting accomplishments. You also minimize the possibility of an uninformed disposition after your death. You might believe that it is harder to spend collectibles than cash and that such a gift will prevent unwise behavior, but the pawnshop story mentioned previously is only one of many that we have encountered over the years.

In summary, your collection is yours to enjoy now and yours to dispose of as you see fit. The old saw says, "You can't take it with you." You can, however, ensure that either the collection, or its proceeds, provide as much positive influence for others as it has for you.

- Make an action plan for your collection, even if you anticipate many more decades of collecting. You can and should continually revise and update your plan periodically. Post-mortem planning is not an option.

- Speak and meet with your advisors to determine which recipient(s), and what method of timing and disposition is most agreeable to you.

- If the timing is immediate, find the advisor or advisors that are essential to the implementation of the plan and proceed accordingly.

– If the timing is later, prepare detailed written instructions and leave copies with both your collection and your will or trust. If you prefer that your collectibles be distributed among family members, provide specific instructions in writing as to how distribution is to be accomplished. If you wish to distribute the proceeds, make certain that you provide directions for non-experts to contact a firm or dealer that is trustworthy, experienced and reputable, to sell the collectibles. Your instructions should be as detailed as possible to accomplish your objectives.

Don't forget to consult with your advisors. Tax laws, and other relevant legislation, are always changing, and it is wise to update your will or trust at least once a year and meet with your team of advisors on a regular basis. It will cost you some money, but good advice will save you much more in the long run than it costs in the short-term.

TIPS FOR HEIRS: This is another chapter that can benefit you only if others read and heed it. You can, however, discuss the relevant issues with your loved ones and share it with them when it seems appropriate. Good communication between family members often avoids the pitfalls of estate planning and eases the transfer of assets. Involvement in a parent's collecting activities may create new and lasting bonds between the family members; you may even begin to enjoy collecting yourself.

King Kong (RKO, 1933).
Austrian Oversize Poster
Sold For: $38,837
November 2010

6

Tax Options for Estate Planning

"The only difference between death and taxes is that death
doesn't get worse every time Congress meets." – Will Rogers

This chapter addresses some of the options available for estate
planning for collections. A collector should use the same care in
planning for their collectible assets as they have for other holdings.
If you are an avid collector, your collection may represent a large
portion of your potential net worth and your estate. While your real
estate, stocks, bonds, and other traditional investments are probably
accounted for in your estate plan, your collection may not be. The
only way that your advisor will know that you have a collection is if
you share that information with him. Even if it is an approximate value,
your advisor will consider these assets in the planning process.

When a person dies owning property, that property is transferred
to a recipient. The process of determining the recipient of assets is
one of the basic concepts of estate planning. Depending upon your
personal circumstances, the decisions you make will have a significant
impact on the amount of ordinary income, capital gains, gift and/or
estate taxes that you or your heirs will pay to Uncle Sam. This chapter
is provided solely to improve your general understanding, as we
cannot know or advise you as to which of these options may apply to
your personal situation or holdings.

We strongly recommend that, after studying this information, you
engage the services of a competent legal professional, preferably
an attorney who is board-certified in estate planning and/or probate
law by your state, and a tax advisor, preferably a CPA who specializes
in taxes. An experienced and competent professional with expertise
in life insurance should also become a valuable part of your team of
advisors.

Feel free to ask as many questions as you need to address your interests and concerns. Between you and your advisory team, you should be able to create the plan that best suits your unique needs and wishes. The tax and estate planning laws are extremely complex and there is no single individual who can be relied upon to advise you on all aspects of the legal, tax and insurance matters that are involved in estate planning. As we stated before, the laws are always changing and have significant impact on the taxation of your estate, and on decisions about the benefits and detriments of making lifetime gifts, or gifts by will or trust. For example, capital gains on collectibles are taxed at a flat rate of 28%, while long term capital gains on other assets, like your stocks or real estate, are generally taxed at the lower rate of 15%.

Annual gifts of up to $13,000 may be made by you to as many individuals as you choose without affecting your lifetime gift exemption. If your wife joins you in the gift, you can distribute $26,000 each year to as many lucky recipients as you choose, without reducing your joint lifetime exemption. In addition, you are allowed, (for 2011 and 2012), a $5,000,000 lifetime gift exemption, $10,000,000 with your spouse, and a generous gift tax exemption for generation-skipping gifts to grandchildren. Unless Congress extends the exemptions, it will revert back to $1,000,000 in 2013.

Taxation should be one (but not the only) factor in developing your long term strategies for your collection.

Is Your Collection Worth More Today Than When You Purchased It?

As with any carefully chosen investment, a collection should hopefully appreciate in value over time. There are, of course, exceptions.

If you were unfortunate enough to have been the victim of an unscrupulous seller, or perhaps acquired some of your collectibles at the peak of a market that has since declined, a current appraisal may indicate that you are in a capital loss position. If that is correct and if imminent disposition is your intention, you may sell the collection and use the loss to offset an equal amount of capital gains. In addition, you may deduct up to $3,000 annually of excess capital losses against your ordinary income. These losses may be carried forward to future years until they are entirely used up, or until your death.

We can't stress this enough: the tax laws are very complex. Certain losses, depending on their character (short or long term) may offset only certain gains and the IRS has established a priority for offsetting short and long term capital gains. However, the $3000 deduction is used against ordinary income rather than to offset capital gains. If you do not have capital gains to offset capital losses, you will still have the ability to deduct $3000 each year against your income tax. The best strategy when you incur capital gains that can't be offset with losses is to simply pay the tax. If the collection has appreciated (which we hope is the case), many other issues come into play. These are discussed over the next few pages.

The Unpredictability of the Estate Tax

Unless you have successfully completed your lifetime planning, many of the assets held directly in your name will transfer into your estate upon your death. Your estate will have to pay estate taxes if the net value is greater than the exemption amount set by Congress. Unfortunately, Congress has made planning for the estate tax challenging by continually changing the amount of the exemptions. Following the Economic Growth and Tax Relief Reconciliation Act of 2001, the estate tax exemption has gradually increased over the last few years culminating in 2010 with a full repeal of any estate tax. For 2011 and 2012, Congress has set the Estate Tax at $5,000,000 exemption and a 35% tax rate. If Congress does not make the tax cuts permanent before 2013, we will see the estate tax returning to a $1,000,000 exemption and 55% tax rate in 2013.

While the erratic nature of the estate tax exemption amounts may be confusing, the consequences of the estate tax are of real concern. If you bequest a large estate of tangible assets to your heirs, without proper planning, your heirs may require a substantial amount of liquid money to satisfy the estate taxes. If there is no estate tax in the year of the estate they may still have to pay significant capital gains taxes if items are sold, as the cost basis of the property would not have been re-established and updated in filings as part of the estate.

Without extensions, estate taxes must be paid to the government in cash within nine months of death. Often, the unfortunate result of this immediate need for cash will be a "fire sale" to raise the required

A Classic Navajo Man's Wearing Blanket
Sold For: $38,240 September 2009

funds by the tax filing date. A hasty sale will not maximize the value of the collection you have devoted a great amount of time and effort to. Despite your best intentions, neither you, nor your children, may benefit from your collection as you had intended without proper advanced planning.

If you are the owner of a substantial collection, it is imperative that you form a strong relationship with an advisor(s) who will assist you in reducing this painful tax liability.

One part of the solution to the need of immediate liquidity to pay for potential estate taxes is through the use of life insurance.

First, you will need your accountant or advisor to develop a pro-forma balance sheet and income statement to determine the extent of the potential tax liability based upon the best estimate of the value of your estate at some future and unknown date. Depending on the valuation of your estate, your advisor can estimate the amount of tax that may be due upon your passing.

This part of your planning is more of an art than a science. The value of your assets, which may appreciate or depreciate over time, is unpredictable and may only be estimated. The date of death is uncertain as are the tax rates that will apply at such time. There are many unknowns, but you have to work with what you have. Your advisor, based on these assumptions, should be able to assist you in determining the tax consequences of making lifetime gifts or making bequests at the time of your passing by will or trust. These assumptions will also determine the various strategies that are available to reduce your tax liabilities.

The amount of life insurance required to pay the estimated tax should be determined in consultation with an insurance advisor as well as your estate planning attorney. As Yogi Berra put it, "Predictions, especially about the future, are hard to make".

A life insurance policy's proceeds do not become part of your estate at death as long as you do not name either yourself or your estate as the beneficiary of the policy, or if the ownership of the policy is held in a separate trust (ILIT) outside of your estate or owned by a third party. The proceeds of the policy are payable immediately in cash and pass to your beneficiaries income tax free. By insuring your life for an amount equal to or in excess of your estimated estate tax liability, you can assure your heirs of sufficient liquidity to discharge the estate taxes, thus enabling the collection to pass to your heirs without requiring them to sell assets. We will explore the benefits of life insurance in planning your estate as we continue to discuss additional strategies.

The Gift Tax and Reducing Your Estate Through Annual Gifting

Especially in light of the onerous estate tax rates that can inflict substantial damage on your estate (remember that potential tax rate of 35-55%), reducing your taxable estate through gifts to your heirs during your lifetime is a simple and extremely advantageous strategy, if implemented properly.

This may be one of the few gifts you will ever receive from our government: It's called the gift tax.

"What," you may ask, "is the gift tax?"

The gift tax applies to transfers of assets during your lifetime to various beneficiaries. Current law allows you to make gifts of present interest to any number of recipients. The donor is responsible for the payment of any taxes that are due on the gift. In general a gift is a transfer of property for less than its full value. In the words of Warren Buffett, "Price is what you pay, value is what you get".

A gift must be accepted by the recipient and is irrevocable. As previously discussed, our current tax law provides for annual gifts of $13,000 per recipient. If your spouse participates (willingly) in the gift, you are allowed to give away $26,000 per year to as many fortunate individuals as you wish. If your gift does not exceed that amount, you do not even have to fill out a tax form for these annual gifts. However, there are limitations. You are also entitled to a one time lifetime gift tax exemption of $5,000,000 per spouse in 2011 and 2012. Once you exceed the annual gift tax limitation of $13,000 per individual, or $26,000 with spouse, two things will happen: You will be required to report the gift to the IRS and it will reduce your lifetime gift tax exemptions dollar for dollar. If you exceed the $5 million or $10 million dollar limitation, you may be subject to the maximum and onerous 35% Federal estate tax rate.

In theory, if you have 10 children and grandchildren (in total), you and your spouse may gift up to $260,000 ($26,000 times 10) each year to them without filing with the IRS. More good things will result. Not only will you make these family members very happy, you will have removed $260,000 from your estate, which is no longer subject to future appreciation and possible estate taxation.

Those who make gifts on a regular annual basis can substantially reduce their estate tax liabilities as long as there are a sufficient number of recipients to make gifts to. Using the above example, in 10 years, it is possible to eliminate $2.6 million dollars from your estate without affecting your lifetime gift tax exemption.

What are the benefits of making gifts as compared to disposing of your assets by will or trust upon your death?

First, there is no downside in using your annual gift tax exemptions as long as it does not deplete your financial resources. However, as discussed, when you exceed your $5 million of lifetime gift tax exemptions, you may subject yourself to that 35% estate tax.

Why would you use the $5 million lifetime exemption - $10 million with your spouse - rather than wait until you pass away and use your estate tax exemptions? The primary reason is that if you use the million dollar exemption to gift property that may appreciate substantially in future years, you will eliminate any future appreciation in these assets from your estate subject to the current (35%) estate tax.

For example, let's say you decide to make a lifetime gift to your daughter of real estate with a fair market value of $5,000,000. When you pass away, many years from now, the real estate is worth $8,000,000. You have reduced your taxable estate (again, think 35%) by $3 million, assuming the property has appreciated by $3 million at the time of your death.

If the same real estate is in your estate when you die and is not a gift, the recipient receives what is known as a stepped up basis in the asset. Basically, if the recipient decides to sell the asset, the basis for determining their gain is determined by the value of the property at the time of your death, which eliminates most of the tax liability if the property is sold soon after you pass away.

The problem is that if you retain the property in your estate when you die, you will be subject to the 35% maximum estate tax. Gifted property usually has what is called a carryover basis. The amount used to determine the gain to the recipient is the original cost of the asset, not the value of the asset at the time of death. So, if you make a five million dollar lifetime gift of real estate with a fair market value of $5,000,000 to your daughter that you purchased for $1,000,000, there will be a capital gain waiting for her of $4,000,000 ($5,000,000 minus $1,000,000).This could be minimized if the property remains in your estate and your assets do not exceed the exemptions.

These stipulated situations apply to 2011 and 2012, and will revert back to pre-2001 levels when the estate tax is reinstated in 2013. Without having an estate tax in 2010, estates do not have to be concerned with the exemption amount or an estate tax rate - though gift tax is still assessed at the highest Individual income tax rate and heirs will have to be concerned with capital gains taxes.

If you do not understand by now why you need expert tax advice, you are either a financial genius or you have not been reading carefully.

Under current law, and we emphasize "current", you may gift an unlimited amount of property during your lifetime to a spouse without paying gift tax as long as your marriage is legally recognized and your spouse is a U.S. citizen. Upon your death, the marital deduction allows you to pass an unlimited amount of property to your spouse tax free. It should be noted that marital transfers merely defer estate taxes, they do not eliminate them. However, by using the marital deduction to equalize the estates of each spouse, it will allow you and your spouse to maximize each of your estate tax exemptions by transferring assets between the two of you. **TALK TO YOUR TAX AND ESTATE PLANNING ADVISOR!**

The use of annual and lifetime gifts is an essential part of any estate plan. It is not exciting, but it is important. At minimum, you now have a basic understanding of the concepts to enable you to ask the appropriate questions of your advisors.

Let's summarize the basic concepts, in the simplest of terms, with the caveat that nothing in this area is simple and legislation is pending that could change many of these rates.

You have a $13,000 annual gift tax exemption that permits gifts to unlimited recipients each year, or $26,000 per year if your spouse joins you. Use this gift to reduce your estate, eliminate appreciation of assets in your estate and enjoy the benefits of generosity. If you have property in your estate that will appreciate, consider using your one time lifetime gift tax exemption of $5 million or $10 million with your spouse, assuming you are comfortable (financially) without the asset. If your estate is estimated at such a value that may trigger the 35% maximum estate tax, one should consider the use of a life insurance trust and a charitable remainder trust to minimize potential taxation. The recipient may incur higher taxes upon the receipt and sale of a gift from you than would be the case if the property was received upon death and sold soon afterwards. There are, though, other strategies to reduce those potential liabilities as well.

The Capital Gains Tax and Like-Kind Exchanges

Almost everything you own for personal or investment purposes is a capital asset. This includes your home, furnishings, stocks held in

GIL ELVGREN (American, 1914-1980)
Bear Facts (A Modest Look; Bearback Rider), 1962
Sold For: $191,200 May 2010

your personal account, and collections.

When you sell a capital asset, the difference between the amount you bought it for and the amount you sold it for (also known as the basis) is a capital gain or capital loss.

If you held the asset for more than a year before selling, it is considered long term. If you held the asset for less than a year, it is short term.

The cost basis of an asset depends upon how you acquired the asset. If you purchased the asset, the basis is the amount you paid at the time of purchase, including but not limited to any associated expenses, such as commissions, fees, and improvements to the property, etc. If you received the property as a gift, the basis is usually the price that the donor making the gift originally paid for it, which is also called the "carry over basis." If you inherited the asset upon the death of the donor, your basis is the fair market value of the asset at the date of death, called a "stepped up basis." If it is received as a gift, the basis is the original purchase price or basis of the donor.

For example, if you are a collector who paid $10,000 for a collection, and at your death the collection is worth $50,000, whoever inherits your collection will have a stepped up basis of $50,000. The effect is to eliminate the $40,000 in gains that you would have incurred. However, you have to die for the gain to be erased; perhaps a high price to pay for some tax savings. Also, the asset that has appreciated will be included in the value of your estate at the appreciated, rather than original, cost.

Capital gains on most assets held for more than one year are taxed at a lower rate than income taxes and are included on your annual income tax return. The capital gains tax is generally 15% on most assets, other than collectibles, that have been held for a year or more. However, the long term capital gains on the sale of collectibles - such as coins, stamps, precious gems, precious metals and rare currency or fine art - taxed at a flat rate of 28%.

This 28% flat tax rate differentiates the tax consequences on the sale of your numismatic objects from other properties which are taxed at a lower rate. Short term gains on objects sold within a one year time frame are taxed at the same rate as your ordinary income tax rate.

Even the most astute of advisors may not be aware of this exception that applies only to collectibles. The consequences of this tax, and its application to collectibles, is critical as there are a number of strategies that may be available to reduce the pain. Do not be deceived by those who may tell you that the tax is only 15% or less. The tax is not progressive, but is still a flat tax imposed on the long term gain at a rate of 28% on the appreciation of the assets.

One strategy to defer long term capital gains taxes on your collectible is to use a Section 1031 like-kind exchange. With this, the tax is not eliminated, but deferred. While a 1031 exchange is commonly used with real estate, it is also applicable to art and other collectibles. The IRS has specifically addressed coins and Section 1031 exchanges and it may be used to defer payment of long term capital gains tax into the future. Only at such time as the replacement property is sold, will the capital gains tax become due. The requirements for these exchanges are extremely technical, but three basic elements are required by the taxing authorities to comply with the regulations:

1. There is an exchange of property that qualifies under Section 1031.

2. The properties exchanged are like-kind to one another.

3. Both properties are held for investment, or used productively in a trade or business.

The first element is clear, but the second one addressing like-kind is more challenging. Like-kind refers to the nature or character of the property, and not its grade or quality.

For example, the IRS has ruled that collectible coins are not like-kind to bullion coins, and that gold bullion is not like-kind to silver bullion. The IRS makes the distinction that the value of numismatic-type coins is determined by their age, the quantity minted, along with history, art and aesthetics, condition, and finally, metal content. On the other hand, the value of bullion coins such as the popular South African Krugerrands is determined solely on the basis of their metal content.

The third element, "held for investment," means that the property was held primarily for profit. The burden of proof falls on the collector to prove that he invested in his collection with the goal of making a profit.

As stressed in previous chapters, the importance of thoroughly documenting your collection cannot be over-emphasized. The IRS will determine the investment purpose by examining your past records. How frequently do you buy and sell your collectibles? What is the profit motive? How much time do you devote to reading catalogs and other materials that enhance your knowledge and investment savvy? Do you travel to shows to gain knowledge of the market or to pursue your hobby? Do you own the type of collectibles that are likely to appreciate? Are the purchases of rare or common coins (stamps, currency)? If you are purchasing low cost, undesirable and common objects, it will be difficult to demonstrate to the IRS that you are an investor and not a hobbyist. It is essential to document all of your activities that will support the argument that you purchased your collectibles with the intention of future price appreciation.

While the concept behind 1031 exchanges is fairly straightforward, the specific rules involving Section 1031 exchanges are more complicated.

Sellers have 45 days to identify their replacement property, and then 180 days to complete the purchase of the new property. If you miss the deadline, the tax break is forfeited. Additionally, the IRS requires that an exchanger use a "qualified intermediary," or a middleman. The purpose of a "QI" is to hold the proceeds of the sale in escrow until the new property is purchased.

The QI is one of four parties in a typical tax deferred exchange. The second is the taxpayer who has property and wants to exchange it for new property. The third is the seller who owns the property that the taxpayer wants to acquire in the exchange. The final party is the buyer who has cash and wants to acquire the taxpayer's property.

Section 1031 exchanges may be a useful tool to defer capital gains taxes when a collection is sold. However, it is essential that a collector receive qualified tax advice and comply with all of the regulations in this area. There is currently legislation before Congress that would exempt collectibles from inclusion in the 1031 exchange, but it has not had any success to this point.

Our concern is regarding the definition of "like kind," and the potential problem that may result if you exchange property or collectibles and it is ruled that they are not like kind as is the case with numismatic and bullion coins.

Are U.S. and foreign coins "like kind"? What about an exchange of paper currency for coins? What about stamps for coins? This is a minefield for possible disaster. Do not proceed without expert tax advice, as there may be other strategies that may be preferable alternatives to the like kind exchange. Remember, taxes are deferred, not eliminated, and there are substantial costs involved in a 1031 exchange regarding fees and other costs. Also, there is always the possibility that the property you receive in the exchange will lose value, while the property that you sell may appreciate.

More Estate Planning Options

Although, other strategies of a more technical nature are outside the scope of this book, there are several other options that may benefit a large estate and minimize gift and estate taxes. As discussed throughout this book, an experienced estate planning attorney, along with your other advisors, can assist in determining which strategy is best for your particular situation.

Trusts

The most commonly used trust is known as "the living trust." In legal terms, it is known as the "revocable living trust." How can a trust be alive?

The use of the living trust has become more popular, and more common, in the last decade. In fact, most banks or lending institutions require their clients to create and fund a living trust.

In simple terms, the living trust is a document that is used in conjunction with a will, but avoids the costs and time involved in probating a will. You transfer your property and title it in the name of the trust.

Example: John Doe, trustee for the John Doe Trust.

Of course, you will need a competent estate planning attorney to draft the documents and explain them to you. A trust is advised for both you and your spouse. A will is only a supplement to the trust that will assure that any assets that have not been transferred into your trust (re-titled) will shift into the trust at the time of your death. Remember, only assets that have been re-titled in the name of the trust will be valid transfers that will accomplish your objectives.

While you are alive, you may be the trustee of your own trust and you will have complete control of the assets during your lifetime. When you pass away, the trustee who you would select (it could be more than one), who is your successor trustee, will step in your shoes and become the new trustee. The new trustee has a fiduciary obligation to follow the terms of the trust as you have stated in the trust document.

A revocable trust, in itself, will not result in specific tax savings and is not a strategy for reducing your gift and estate tax liabilities, nor your capital gains issues. However, it will avoid the expense (legal and other), the time and the publicity of Probate involved in leaving only a will.

While the terms of a will are public knowledge, the terms of a trust are private, and within the control of you and the parties that you select to be involved in the process. Assets will be transferred soon after death, legal fees will be minimized and the terms will remain private. Also, there is far less risk of an unhappy family member contesting a trust as compared to a will.

There will be ancillary tax benefits. The trust will provide for the disposition of your assets in accordance with your wishes. In addition, the trust will permit you to take full advantage of the marital deduction and your tax exemptions by designating the exact proportion of assets to be distributed and the specific recipients.

This is a summary only and an expert is required to properly draft the trust and other ancillary documents. It is common to include in your planning specific provisions that will apply if you become disabled, terminally ill or require medical attention. State your intention should you be on life support and unable to make medical and other decisions.

One of the other major benefits of a living trust is that it will contain directions for the trustee as to your care, and the protection of your assets, should you be unable to make such decisions due to your health or mental condition. Your designated trustee will assume control of your property and make the necessary decisions rather than a probate judge.

One last thing, do not leave home without one!

There is also an AB trust, commonly called a QTIP (Qualified Terminable Interest Property), bypass trust or a marital trust, where spouses leave property in trust for their children, but provide the surviving spouse with the right to use the property or income from the property for his or her lifetime. The AB trust maximizes the deceased spouse's personal exemption (currently that aforementioned $5,000,000 in 2011). The result, if properly executed, is the ability to take full advantage of the total of $10,000,000 of estate exemptions allowed to both spouses based on the current tax law exemption for 2011 which will surely change in the coming years.

A QTIP trust permits a spouse to transfer assets to their trust while maintaining control over the disposition of those assets upon the death of the spouse. These trusts are common in second marriages where a person desires assurance that the children from the first marriage will receive assets which could conceivably go to children from the second marriage to their exclusion. Irrevocable life insurance trusts are often used because - as mentioned before in this chapter - life insurance proceeds are not taxable unless the ownership of the policies are in your name or the estate is the beneficiary of the policy. You can transfer a small amount, equal to the life insurance premium, to an irrevocable life insurance trust through your heirs and use of your annual gifts, which will reduce the size of your taxable estate while creating a much larger asset (the life insurance proceeds) that remains outside of the estate.

As an heir to a taxable estate, once the donor or owner of the collectible has passed away, most of your opportunities to reduce the estate tax consequences will have passed. If you have access to the will or trust of your parent (or other person to whom you may become an heir), perhaps you are able to advise the person to seek counsel to draft the necessary documents.

If it is necessary to liquidate all or part of the collection to pay estate taxes, the expenses of that liquidation (shipping, insurance, auction fees, commissions, etc.) are generally deductible from the

Property of a Southern California Estate
DAUM FRERES
'Rain' landscape vase with shaped lip,
patterned on both faces, circa 1900
Sold For: $14,340 December 2010

estate. Additionally, estate expenses related to the use of lawyers and probate costs are deductible from the total gross estate. It is still advantageous to arrange your estate plan to reduce these expenses rather than to deduct them (see living trust).

If you are the surviving spouse of the deceased, exemptions generally allow the estate to pass to you without tax being owed. The estate planning burden then becomes yours, however, as the same exemptions will not apply at your death unless you remarry. If this eventuality was not already considered in your planning, you should contact an estate or tax professional without delay. Even if the survivor's estate Issues were considered in the original planning, it cannot hurt to re-evaluate the situation with a trusted advisor.

Life Insurance and Taxes

Although, most of us have certain suspicions regarding insurance advisors, the truth is that life insurance is one of the most valuable tools available, in the hands of a competent tax expert, under our current tax structure.

Woody Allen once said, "There are worse things in life than death. Have you ever spent an evening with an insurance salesman?"

Times have changed. The days of Arthur Miller's tragic Willy Loman are over! Insurance advisors, those who are associated with major insurance concerns, are required to have a clear understanding, not only of their products but the many uses of life insurance for estate planning. Many are well trained and are as expert in their field as are attorneys, doctors and accountants.

Life insurance is afforded a number of tax advantages that are unavailable with other forms of investments. It is highly leveraged. If you die after the initial premium has been paid, you will receive a large multiple of that amount in cash, and as Yogi Berra says, or may have said, "It's also liquid."

An expert insurance advisor is a critical component of your estate planning team. Ideally, long-term life insurance should be purchased while you are young and healthy. The same benefits may not be available should you become ill or incapacitated. Do not wait until you are in poor health, or when you are at such an age when the costs of insurance are prohibitive.

There are two primary uses of life insurance in the estate planning process where the estate is substantial enough to incur taxation at the maximum current rate.

The first use is to provide liquidity necessary should there be an untimely death and your estate is significant enough to be subject to the estate tax. Such life insurance must be held outside of your estate. The IRS will want its money right away.

Remember, not all insurance proceeds are excluded from your estate: If you are the owner of the policy or you name either yourself or your estate as the beneficiary, the proceeds will be included in the valuation of your estate upon death. Pardon our repetition, but it's so critical to understand this concept, and the other basic ones we've discussed, so that your advisor can be helpful in assuring that the life insurance proceeds remain outside of your estate.

Another important use for life insurance is to replace assets that you may donate during your lifetime, or upon your death, to charity, with the proceeds of life insurance that will remain outside of your estate. Since your heirs will lose any benefit from the donated property, you may use the tax deductions to purchase life insurance and make them the beneficiaries of the life insurance proceeds.

Many collectors have heard of an ILIT and have no idea of what it is. In legalese, an ILIT is an acronym for an Irrevocable Life Insurance Trust. It is a method of eliminating the ownership of an insurance policy from your estate while deriving all of the tax free benefits that apply to your beneficiaries. If drafted properly and funded appropriately, the proceeds of the policy will not be included in your estate and your heirs will receive a large sum of money (liquidity) with which to pay your estate tax liabilities. It will also replace the asset that is being donated to charity if you have created a Charitable Remainder Trust (CRT) and the heirs will not receive the property that is going to charity. However, the trust and the method of payment must be strictly adhered to for this process to achieve these objectives. The life insurance policy will be owned by an irrevocable trust, which is a separate document from your living trust. As stated, the goal is for the proceeds to avoid taxation on your estate and to avoid probate, while providing your heirs with liquidity to quickly pay any of the estate tax liabilities.

The first step is to hire an attorney who is an expert in estate planning and taxation to draft the documents. Be forewarned, the trust is irrevocable; it cannot be modified once the assets have been transferred.

The next step is to find an insurance advisor with experience, and expertise, in estate planning and life insurance. Once you have determined the amount of insurance that will be required - and this can only be an estimate, as property values changes, as do family members - you will do one of two things: If you have an existing policy, if it is suitable, it may be transferred into the trust. If an existing policy is used, you must live for a minimum of three more years to avoid the estate tax. This is risky, for you and the tax issue. The alternative is to have the trust purchase a new policy on your life under which you can pass away the next day with all of the tax benefits intact. Such an option is preferable if you are in good health and insurable, which leads us to the next step.

If the estate is structured properly, the tax burden will fall primarily on the estate of the last spouse to die. As a result of the unlimited marital deduction and the maximum use of exemptions, the bulk of your estate will go to your spouse and vice-versa. To reduce the cost of the life insurance and to provide the liquidity for the estate taxes, it makes sense to insure the last to die.

Assuming that both spouses are alive, most advisors will recommend that you purchase a whole life insurance policy on both spouses that will pay when the last spouse passes away. This is known as a "last to die" policy. No further explanation is necessary.

There is one more problem: Who should pay the premiums on the policy? The correct answer is critical to your estate planning and necessary to avoid further taxation. The heirs are the likely source for the payment of the premiums.

Why? Because your heirs will be the beneficiaries of your generosity. How, though, do they find the money to pay the premiums? Do you remember the annual gift tax? You are going to give your heirs the money to pay the insurance on your life that will provide them with their inheritance. That sounds like a great plan, right? At least for them if not for you.

In fact, most collectors should use the annual gift tax exemption to give your heirs an amount that will cover the cost of the premiums. Remember, you can make annual gifts of $13,000 or $26,000 if your spouse joins you. You are essentially purchasing a life insurance policy to benefit your heirs while a the same time giving them cash gifts with which to pay the premiums. Life (insurance) is not always fair.

There is also another word of caution:

These gifts must be gifts of "present interest" to qualify for the annual gift tax exemption; ask your attorney. To qualify for the exclusion, you must give the heirs the right to reject the gift, usually for a period of 30 days. That creates a present gift. These gifts will be transferred to the trust where, as we discussed, the funds will be used to pay for the life insurance premiums. The factors that make this a present rather than future gift are known as the "Crummey powers." They are well named after a taxpayer who argued to the IRS that these annual gifts are gifts of present interest. One last problem: There are many forms of life insurance.

There are whole life policies, term policies, universal life, variable life policies and many, many more. Without going into a detailed study of life insurance, be forewarned: DO NOT, UNDER ANY CIRCUMSTANCES, USE TERM LIFE INSURANCE TO FUND THE TRUST. Use a form of whole life insurance. Term insurance may be cheaper, but it may expire before you do and will have no benefit in terms of funding the policy if it is no longer in effect when you pass away. It is a good idea, in certain circumstances, but not in funding an ILIT, and for estate planning purposes.

Whole life insurance, whether variable or universal life, or other permanent insurance, should be used to assure that the funds will be available should you live to be 120 years old. Also, when term insurance expires, you may not be insurable and term insurance premiums increase exponentially after age 60. A whole life policy will cover the last to die. There may be exceptions to this rule, so speak with your advisor if term life is recommended for the ILIT.

In addition, the trust will have the ability to borrow from the cash value of a whole life policy. For other needs without income tax consequences. Variable life policies actually allow the trustee to invest the cash value in a number of investments, such as mutual funds and bond funds (but not art or collectibles). These investments can be transferred within the policy from fund to fund without any tax consequences, which is an attractive benefit. However, should these investments go down, there may be additional cash required to maintain the policy benefits.

TIPS FOR HEIRS: An ILIT is an important planning tool that provides liquidity to pay for any estate tax liabilities; the proceeds are not included in your estate. You may gift the premium amounts to your heirs using the annual gift tax exclusion and the proceeds will be received tax free to your heirs to be used to pay the estate taxes and all's well that ends well. It is important that the documents are drafted properly by an expert and the gifts are made in accordance with IRS rulings. Insurance is a critical part and strategy of any substantial estate. Make an expert a part of your team.

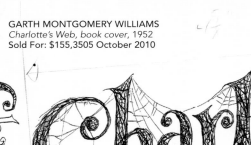

7

Collectibles and Charitable Giving

"In faith and hope the world will disagree, But all mankind's
concern is charity." – Alexander The Great

"To give requires good sense." – Ovid

The nonprofit sector provides a source of deep meaning in our
national life by enhancing our creativity and our communities.
In 2005, for example, $260,000,000,000 was donated to charitable
causes by the U.S. taxpayer alone. Individuals donated almost
$200,000,000,000 of that.

People are charitable for a variety of reasons. Many are motivated
by purely charitable reasons, others seek public acknowledgment.
While you may not be charitable by nature, a charitable gift can be
used in conjunction with other strategies to reduce or eliminate taxes.
Tax laws provide benefits to those who donate in order to encourage
greater donations. Charitable tax deductions share the cost of operat-
ing these institutions that provide essential functions. For example,
charitable tax deductions support religious organizations, educational
institutions, hospitals, museums, wildlife, and human aid, among
many things.

Charitable Giving Nuts and Bolts

For tax purposes, a charitable gift makes the most sense when a
collection has incurred substantial capital gains from appreciation. As
a general rule, property that is today valued for less than what was
paid should be sold at a loss rather than donated to charity, as this
generates a section 165 loss deduction, which may result in a deduction that is greater than a charitable deduction in many cases.

However, the amount of your deduction is based upon the fair
market cost of the property and not the original cost to you. If you

give a gift, to the appropriate charity, with a fair market value of $50,000 that originally cost $10,000, you will receive a deduction for the entire $50,000. This is the benefit of a charitable donation that has appreciated in value. When looking at the tax implications of a charitable gift, it is imperative that you involve your tax planner and attorney and advisors, as the rules in this area, as defined by the Internal Revenue Code, are complicated.

If your collection has appreciated, you may be able to enjoy some fiscal benefit through a charitable donation to a public charity. Here is what it takes to qualify:

1. The donated items are qualified capital gains property

This generally means that the donated items have been in the collection for at least a year, are not tangible items created by you (because if they were, you would only be allowed to deduct the cost of materials in most cases), nor was it a gift from the creator. The latter two portions of the qualifications are based on art law; however, if you are considering medallic art (such as tokens or medals), or other privately issued exonumia (such as items related to coin production), those rules may apply.

2. The donee organization is a qualified public charity

Public charities generally receive at least part of their support from the public. IRS Section 501(c)(3) lists the types of donee organizations and the guidelines for them to follow to qualify for the charitable deduction. The charity must serve a public, rather than a private, interest and must meet an "organizational test."

Additionally, the organization must be organized and operated for a religious, charitable, scientific, literary, or educational purpose.

For example: Churches, schools and museums are generally considered to be qualified public charities, while private foundations are not. The difference is that you receive a deduction based only upon the actual cost of the donated item when it concerns a private foundation, while a public charitable donation can be deducted at full fair market value. It is reasonable for a potential donor to request that an organization write a letter confirming that the IRS has made a determination that the organization qualifies for tax-exempt status under

Section 501(c)(3), and that the charity intends to use the objects for a valid charitable purpose.

3. The donee organization must make "related use" of the donation

Your gift of tangible personal property must relate to the exempt purposes or functions of the organization. For example, if you donate a coin collection to the American Numismatic Society for the purpose of expanding its museum collections, you would receive a deduction of fair market value since the collection relates to the Society's mission of increasing the knowledge and enjoyment of coin collecting.

If you now donate that collection to a hospital that intends to sell the collection and use the revenue for its capital campaign, you cannot deduct the fair market value, only your acquisition cost of the items. The difference between types of use is subjective and often confusing, so it is important to determine the use for the gift.

An additional factor, which reinforces the importance of communicating with the charity, is that a charitable deduction for contributions of tangible personal property exceeding $5,000 must be reduced or recaptured if the donee sells the property for less than your deducted amount within three years of the contribution.

Also, make sure that the qualified organization actually wants the donation. The organization should provide a written acceptance of the collection or item, stating that they are a qualified public charity and that the donation satisfies the related use rule.

4. The collection has a "qualified appraisal"

The IRS requires a qualified appraisal if the gift is more than $5,000. If the gift is greater than $20,000, a complete copy of the signed appraisal must be attached to the tax return.

A qualified appraisal is defined by the IRS; your advisor should be familiar with these requirements. A qualified appraiser is an individual who holds himself out to the public as an appraiser and has earned an appraisal designation from a recognized professional organization or has otherwise met certain education and experience requirements, regularly performs appraisals for compensation, and meets any other such requirements prescribed by IRS.

Other Issues Relevant in Charitable Giving

Most charities know very little about collectible assets. If you want your donation to be a meaningful contribution, you have to determine that the charity will use your collection to fulfill its intended purpose.

In most cases, that means that it will have to sell your collection to raise funds. Unless you are donating the collection to a museum that will display it or use it for research, it is probably best to dispose of it in your lifetime while you are able to enjoy the good works that the donation can create. If you cannot tolerate the idea of selling your collection, then you should leave detailed written instructions for the disposition of your gift. As wonderful as charities are, they are likely to have less affection for your collection than an heir, and a greater interest in putting your donation to good use by converting it to cash.

In light of these concerns, an auction is a popular choice. It is imperative that you select an auctioneer with experience in your field. The charity of choice can be named as beneficiary of the proceeds from the auction. Assisting your charity in planning for the sale of your collection ensures that the charity will receive the maximum return without exhausting its own resources.

Limitations and the Five-Year Carry Over

What if you donate a very large item that results in a very large tax deduction relative to your income level?

The IRS presently limits the amount of a charitable income tax deduction to a percentage of current income. If the donation is made to a qualified public charity, and the gift is considered a related use, you can deduct the current fair market value up to 30% of your adjusted gross income. If the donation is made to a qualified public charity, but is a non-related use, then your deduction is limited to your cost basis up to 50% of your adjusted gross income. However, you can carry forward the excess deductions for up to five years, until the amount is fully deducted.

For example, a collector with an adjusted gross income of $100,000 has a coin that he purchased for $50,000 in 1985; it is now worth $150,000. The collector donates it to the ANS who plans to exhibit it. Because the donation is to a qualifying organization and is a related use, he can deduct the fair market value of $150,000, subject to a limit of 30% of his current adjusted gross income. Therefore, in the current year he is able to deduct $30,000 and can carry forward the remaining $120,000 in deductions over the next four years.

Donating a Fractional Interest

Fractional giving is a process where you donate percentages of ownership of a collection or single object over a multi-year time frame. The percentage that you donate is the percentage that you can receive as a charitable tax deduction. Historically, it benefited public institutions while it allowed the donors both estate and capital gains tax deductions. It provided the added benefit of allowing the donor to retain possession for a period of time and the affiliation of the collection with the museum has the potential to increase the collection's value (and increase the charitable tax deduction).

The Pension Protection Act of 2006 directs donors to gift the entire interest in the collection to the charity within 10 years of the initial donation, or death, whichever comes first. Also, the donee institution must maintain substantial physical possession of the object within 10 years of the initial contribution.

The penalties imposed for non-compliance of the guidelines are harsh: one could lose the tax deduction and incur a 10% penalty. Finally, the 2006 law which modified the method of how the gift is valued, causes a harsh result if you initiate the fractional giving process when the collection is going down in value. In the past, if the value of the donated objects increased over time, the donor was allowed a larger deduction based on the appreciated value. Now, the value is frozen at the time of the donation rather than in the future.

Recent proposals include changes to the 2006 law and suggest such changes as a 20 year period for completing the donation, required statements of value from the IRS, allowed revaluation of value during the period of the gift and commensurate physical possession of the donated material commensurate with the ownership percentage. Until Congress changes the laws affecting this area, fractional gifts may be a very difficult estate planning option. Collectors who are considering making fractional gifts should obtain expert advice prior to gifting.

Charitable Remainder Trusts-Overview

A charitable remainder trust (CRT) is beneficial if you want both income and a tax deduction, and are prepared to give up your collection now.

It is particularly advantageous if the collection has enjoyed significant appreciation since the time of acquisition, and you are no longer emotionally attached to it. In this arrangement, the donation is made to the qualifying charity in trust. The charity agrees to pay you annually, either a fixed amount of money (annuity trust) or a percentage of the trust's total value (unitrust) for life, or for a set number of years (not to exceed 20).

The benefit is that if you sold the collection yourself to create income, the principal amount would be reduced by the taxes on the capital gains (28%). In a CRT, the trustee can sell the collection tax free and create a larger principal base. You can claim the collection's future or reminder value (based on IRS tables) as a charitable deduction in the year that the property is transferred to the trust because the trust is considered a "non-related use." You receive your agreed-upon payments and when the trust period is complete, all remaining interest in the trust passes to the charity with both you and the institution avoiding capital gains taxes on the appreciated value of the items. Ultimately, you receive a regular income stream, while avoiding estate taxes and probate by transferring the asset out of the estate.

There are some caveats. Most collectibles are not "income-producing assets," so the collection - at least most of it - may have to be sold in the first year of the trust to fund it with qualifying financial vehicles. The annual distribution to the donor must be a minimum of 5% of the trust's value and a maximum of 50%. Additionally, at the conclusion of the agreement, the remainder to the qualified charity must be at least 10% of the initial value. These rules are subject to change, and create a certain amount of latitude in the trust agreement that must be negotiated between the donor and the charity. Again, we strongly recommend that you use the services of a competent estate planning attorney or tax advisor.

1913 5C Liberty PR64 NGC.
The Olsen Specimen
Sold For: $3,737,500
January 2010

CHARITABLE REMAINDER TRUSTS-
The Real Deal

A charitable remainder trust is a gift that keeps on giving. This may be one of the few gifts that you may ever receive from the IRS. Where else in the Internal Revenue Code are you able to make a charitable donation, receive an immediate tax deduction which may be carried forward, if necessary, reduce your estate and estate tax while you receive an income for a period of years without paying? You guessed it: The 28% capital gain on the appreciation of your collectibles. This is tax relief on steroids.

While the government decided to impose a long term capital gain of 28% on collectibles, it has included collectibles among the charitable tax advantages available to property, such as real estate, that is taxed at lower capital gain rates.

Listen carefully:

First, revisit your tax advisor. Trusts are very complex legal documents that must be drafted properly or you may lose all of the potential tax benefits. An expert is required to avoid future distress. The trust is irrevocable and once property is transferred only a few minor changes are permitted without harmful results. Have them establish a charitable remainder trust. There are a number of variations known as CRATs, CRUTs, and GRUTs. See if they know their stuff. At the time that you transfer your collectibles to the trust, you will be entitled to an immediate tax deduction on your income tax. Retain a qualified appraiser, who is familiar with the IRS qualifications, and an appraisal to support the value of the property.

The IRS, as we will discuss, has strict rules regarding the qualifications for a qualified appraiser and appraisal. The amount of the deduction is the fair market (not the actual cost) value of the assets discounted over the length of the trust assuming that you have owned these objects for more than one year.

The length of the trust may be term certain (not to exceed 10 years) or it may continue over the term of your life, or the lives of you and your spouse. The longer the term of the trust, the less the charitable deduction. For example, the trust distributions may endure for a maximum of 20 years, or for the rest of your life, or for the rest of yours and your spouse's life.

The amount of the immediate deduction may only offset only 30% of your adjusted gross income in the first year, however, if the deduction cannot be fully used in the first year, it may be carried forward for up to five years. The trust is tax exempt and is able to sell appreciated assets without incurring any capital gains. This means that the full sale proceeds (not just the after-tax portion can be invested to generate an annual income for life for yourself and/or your spouse.

Here is what this means. If you sold your collection today for $3 million, and you paid $1 million for it 10 years ago, you would pay the 28% capital gain, which would leave you with a $560,000 tax bill.

The net amount available for investment would be $2,440,000 ($3,000,000 less the $560,000 tax) that you could invest as you may determine. However, the trust will be able to invest the entire $3,000,000 and provide you with an income for life, or lives, or up to 20 years at a rate that the donor (you) determines with the charity. The asset is now out of your estate and no longer subject to estate taxes, which - remember, is currently 35% straight to Uncle Sam, depending on your exemptions.

The only other rules are that the annual distributions from the trust must be a minimum of 5% of the value, and a maximum of 50%. Also, at the time the trust ends, the remainder that goes to the charity must be at least 10% of the initial value of the contribution.

This is the ideal solution for the collector whose collection has substantially appreciated in value and is now subject to the 28% capital gain, , who would like to sell his collection and does not have heirs that have an interest in owning the collectibles.

The other, less favorable, alternative is to retain the collection until you die whereupon your heirs will receive a stepped up basis if they sell the assets. The assets, though, will be included in the value of the estate, which may in itself create a tax if exemptions do not preclude estate taxation at the time of death.

The easiest and most understandable way to explain the charitable remainder trust concept is by way of example. We will use real estate, although the capital gains tax is currently 15%, which is much less than the 28% for collectibles. The theory is the same and you can understand the positive results:

Martha Smith is 75 years old.

She owns 500 shares of BP that are worth $100,000 today.

The shares were purchased for $20,000 15 years ago.

She does not want to pay the 15% capital gains (28% if collectibles).

She establishes a CRAT, charitable remainder annuity trust. She transfers the stock into the trust.

The CRAT sells the stock to and invests the proceeds into high yielding investments.

The CRAT pays no tax on the capital gain when the assets are sold.

The CRAT pays Martha 10% of the net fair market value of the trust annually for the rest of her life. The return may be negotiated subject to guidelines.

The CRAT pays Martha $10,000 in the first year - $100,000 times 10%. She will receive this amount every year until she dies. If she has a spouse, it would continue for both of their lives or a set period up to 10 years from the date of transfer of the assets.

Martha receives an immediate tax deduction of $41,119.

Martha uses her large deduction to purchase a life insurance policy to transfer into her ILIT with her heirs as beneficiaries.

Martha will gift enough money to her heirs each year using her annual exclusion of $12,000 to pay the insurance premiums.

The heirs will pay the amount to the trust that is needed for the life insurance premiums.

The $100,000 of BP is no longer in Martha's estate

The heirs will receive the proceeds from the life insurance, tax free, and go on a vacation or buy a new Bentley.

In essence, Martha will not have to pay any of the capital gains tax on the appreciation of the assets, she will have an immediate tax deduction of $41,119, she will receive $10,000 per year for her life and the stock is no longer part of her estate subject to the estate tax. In fact, she has basically eliminated or diminished both potential estate and capital gains taxes. If she had a spouse, she and her spouse could choose to receive income for the rest of both of their lives.

There is also a vehicle known as a NIMCRUT, which is a variation of a CRT that will allow the trust to make up distributions that it could not pay from earnings on the investments of the trust. If the trust has agreed to pay 6% per year to the donor, or donors, and there is not sufficient income from the investments to pay the full amount, it has the ability to make up the difference to the donor by the time the trust terminates. These funds could be used for retirement purposes as part of your retirement plan.

TIPS TO HEIRS: In summary, when it comes to charitable planning and your collection, there are many options available to you, each with specific benefits and pitfalls. However, the laws are so complex in the area of charitable giving that often, the most seasoned tax professional may not understand the full implications of a charitable gift. When considering making a charitable gift, it is extremely important that you collaborate with your advisory team and the charitable institution to ensure that your gift will provide both you and the organization with the maximum benefits.

The Black Cat (Universal, 1934).
Sold For: $334,600 November 2009

PART THREE

Evaluating Your Collection

8

Third Party Authentication and Grading of Coins

Authenticity and evaluation are vital matters for any collection. This chapter concentrates on third-party grading services that are available to grade and authenticate your collectibles. These services are widely available for coins, sports cards and comics. Use them as needed, but consider the cost, quality and value of grading services for your collectibles. For many items, especially lesser-valued pieces, grading may not be necessary.

For coin grading, the American Numismatic Association (ANA) adopted Sheldon's 70-point grading system and, between 1973 and 1977, worked to establish standards for all series under the leadership of numismatic luminary Abe Kosoff. Experts from all coin specialties collaborated with Mr. Kosoff to develop the first official ANA grading guide, published in 1978.

Initially, it recognized three grades to evaluate Mint State coins: Uncirculated or MS-60; Choice Uncirculated or MS-65; and Perfect Uncirculated or MS-70. Unfortunately, the third grade (MS-70) was mostly theoretical, and the two remaining designations quickly proved inadequate for the marketplace. MS-63 (Select Uncirculated) and MS-67 (Gem Uncirculated) were added to the system and functioned successfully for a period of time until the demand for closer evaluation required additional grades. Eventually, all numbers between MS-60 and MS-70 were employed and the adjectival equivalents were eliminated.

NGC and PCGS remain the acknowledged leaders for coin grading. The reason for their success is that they are the only firms that have maintained sufficient dealer confidence to allow coins to be traded routinely on a sight-unseen basis. As such, while we will list the contact information for several grading services in the Appendix, we will address only NGC and PCGS in the text.

Comics and cards are generally graded on a 10 point scale, with a '10' being the highest grade (most perfect quality). Several grading services are listed for these collectible categories in the Appendix. For comics, Comics Guaranty, LLC (CGC) is recognized as the most trusted grading service. Heritage Comics (HA.com) offers a discount off of standard CGC grading costs, and more information can be obtained from the company Web site.

Sports card authenticity is often entrusted to one of three major grading houses: Professional Sports Authenticator (PSA), Beckett Grading Services (BGS) and Sportscard Guaranty LLC (SGC). Talk to your local card dealers, or find one online, and ask which grading service has the most credibility among the dealers and collectors. Collectors of Sports and Celebrity autographed items use PSA/DNA to authenticate their collectibles. They, too, are listed in the Appendix to this book.

Stamp collectors frequently rely on the grading services of Professional Stamp Experts (PSE). The PSE Web site (see Appendix) contains detailed instructions and an online submission kit, both of which are excellent guides on how to properly submit stamps for grading.

What Should You Certify?

Certification is an expensive proposition that should be approached with caution. At $15-$85 an item, the total costs, for even a small collection, can easily run into the thousands of dollars. Not all collectibles benefit equally from being certified. The rule of thumb, of course, is that the finished product has to be worth more than the raw (ungraded) item, plus the certification fee. Just what does that mean?

There are two practical reasons to certify a collectible: To determine authenticity and to add value.

When a dealer considers buying an uncertified collectible, he is trying to guess how the grading service is going to grade it, always giving himself the benefit of the doubt in case of error. For example, if a dealer is looking at your 1886-O Morgan dollar and he is trying to decide whether NGC will grade it an MS-63 (valued at, say, $3,000) or MS-64 (valued at $7,800), he will designate it as an MS-63 coin to be on the safe side, and offer a price commensurate with an MS-63 coin.

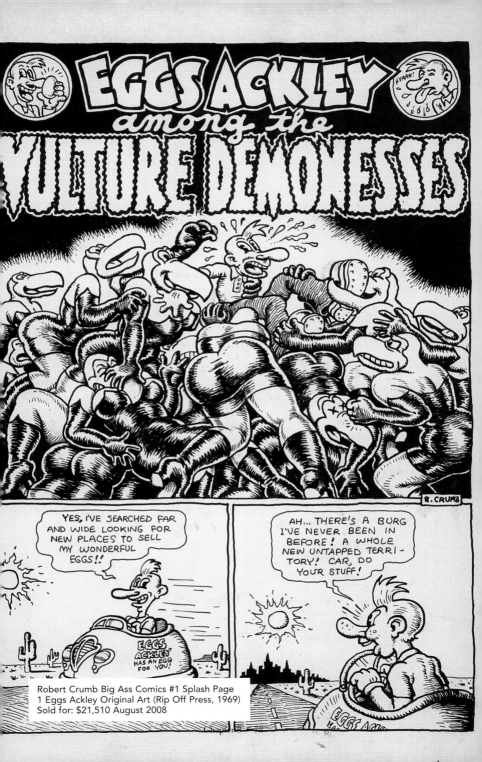

This is only fair, as the alternative would leave him with both the risk and the expense, and that is not a formula for success. You could, however, have the coin certified before attempting to sell it. Your upside is that if the grading service calls it an MS-64, you have a $7,800 coin. The downside is the cost of the grading fee. The bottom line is that this issue has a significant value spread between grades and - in our opinion - the risk is worth the expense.

Submitting Your Coins

NGC and PCGS both operate primarily through authorized dealer networks. Most of these dealers will frequently submit your coins to their respective grading services on your behalf. The dealer is often compensated with a rebate of approximately 20% of the grading fee. Don't request part of the rebate, but do ask him to preview the coins and help you determine which coins to submit for certification. Most authorized dealers are familiar with the standards of both grading services and can help keep you from submitting coins that are most likely targeted for a "body bag" due to damage.

If you reside within driving distance of an authorized dealer, make an appointment to preview the coins with them. If you are not within a reasonable distance, you may ship your coins to an authorized dealer of your choice. As this situation adds an additional element of trust, you should select a dealer or expert who you believe to be trustworthy. A good rule of thumb is to select an authorized dealer who is also a member of the Professional Numismatists Guild (PNG). The PNG is the most prestigious numismatic fraternal organization and each new candidate must undergo a detailed background check and be approved by the entire membership. They must then conduct themselves under a strict Code of Ethics and submit to binding arbitration in the event of disputes. Contact information for the PNG is also included in the Appendix.

Declaring Submission Value for Insurance

When you prepare to submit your collectibles for grading, you will be requested to declare a value for insurance purposes. This is important should the package become lost or the items damaged in transit or at the grading service. Since grading and shipping fees are both impacted by this decision, you need to determine whether the value ranges of the service is commensurate with the likelihood of loss or damage, then select a liberal, yet realistic value for the items.

Third party grading is of major benefit to assist you and your heirs in the estate planning process. Knowing that your coins are protected and identified as well as graded is not only a comfort, but will ease the burden of appraising the collectibles. Certification by a reputable grading system will increase the liquidity of your collection when it is sold. Certified coins are easy to trade among dealers, and on the Internet, to a large number of potential collectors, dealers and auctions. Your heirs and advisors will not have to devote the necessary time to catalog and identify your collection.

Third Party Grading will protect your collectibles, allow your heirs to value and identify them and provide liquidity when the collection is sold.

TIPS FOR HEIRS: As a non-collector, items for third party grading and authentication for the important items in your inheritance will provide you and your heirs with a far greater comfort level in assessing the real value of the collection. Because you are probably unfamiliar with the "language" of the hobby, not to mention the nuances, we recommend that you devote additional time in qualifying the authorized dealer you consult. Speak plainly about your goals and ask a lot of questions. If you are not satisfied with the responses to your questions, don't hesitate to request a more detailed explanation. You cannot learn enough about your inheritance; only knowing too little can hurt you.

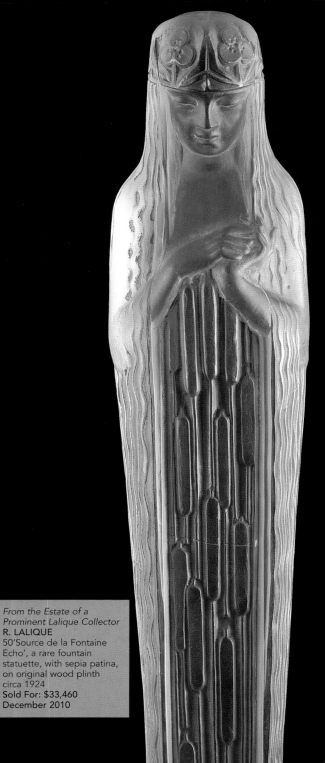

9

Having Your Collection Appraised

Appraisals of collectibles and other tangible personal property are an integral component of estate planning. Appraisals are required for estate tax, charitable contributions and gift tax purposes as well as for insurance and divorce settlements.

A key element in the process is the selection of an appraiser. In rare coins, for instance, the appraiser must be familiar with trends in the entire rare coin market as well as the individual specialization areas they may have in order to provide accurate appraisals that can be submitted to the IRS.

Most rare coins are easier to evaluate than other forms of tangible assets as a result of the vast empirical database that exists. U.S. rare coins have independent pricing guides that are published weekly, along with recognized, independent certification services and a strong established auction history. However, some rare coins are rather esoteric and require a skilled appraiser to evaluate the factors of provenance, rarity, variety, type, quality and, where uncertified coins are involved, the condition based on contemporary standards.

Appraising art and paper collectibles (rare books, comics, and art) often requires an appraiser with a trained eye for the works of particular artists and a comprehensive understanding of the current market for those particular genres of the collectibles. It may be necessary to speak with several appraisers before choosing one with the particular expertise that is required. Heritage Auctions Appraisal Services (HA. com/appraise) can assist you with finding a qualified appraiser either from our in-house experts or from an independent professional.

It is also important that the appraiser is aware of the IRS rules governing appraisals as set forth in the Internal Revenue Code, the Treasury regulations promulgated under the Code and interpreting authority. Neither the IRS nor Congress has yet sought to unify the appraisal requirements for income tax, estate tax or gift tax purposes. Crucial differences exist, such as (1) the requirement that certain estate tax, but not income tax or gift tax appraisals, be made under oath, and (2) the minimum values (e.g. $5,000 and $20,000), above which special appraisal requirements apply.

As a result, in obtaining an appraisal to be used for tax purposes, you should be careful to express clearly the tax purpose that the appraisal is to be used for. In addition, you should review the draft appraisal for compliance with the specific requirements.

Each party involved in the process will have different motivations to either increase or lower the appraised values. For gifts and estate tax purposes, lower appraised valuations are preferred by the taxpayer. However, for transfers to a charitable trust, a higher valuation may increase the deduction and benefit the taxpayer. Higher valuations may affect the limitations imposed upon annual gift tax rules on the lifetime gift tax exemptions. The IRS will contend otherwise should a dispute arise, so the appraisal must be able to withstand close scrutiny, which is one of the reasons an appraiser must swear under oath and is subject to certain penalties in respect to the fairness and accuracy of the appraisal.

For professionals in the appraisal business, the subtitle of this chapter might be "How the Antiques Roadshow Confuses Everyone."

We love the Antiques Roadshow, of course, and as auctioneers serving collectors, we are very grateful for all the Roadshow has done to raise public awareness about – and enthusiasm for – collecting. By necessity, though, the show oversimplifies: Fast, verbal descriptions of inconsistent value types, with all of the effort and intensive research edited out, appearing to flow extemporaneously from the mouths of apparently brilliant television personalities, all protected by the "entertainment-only" waiver protection that such shows enjoy.

One participant is told a value "in my retail shop," and another is told "at auction the estimate would be," and yet others are told "you might take home 'x' amount of dollars" for this item. Many different definitions of value are expressed without any basis or explanation for their differences and viewers at home are left with the presumption that all appraisals can be successfully completed in 20-second sound bites.

Finally, there is the "I-saw-one-just-like-it-on-Antiques-Roadshow" effect, encountered by professional appraisers everywhere, who are expected or forced to explain why and how their client's item is not the same or similar to the one they saw on television. Humor aside, a formal, "qualified appraisal" is a much more serious matter, with wide ranging financial and legal repercussions.

The verbal evaluation option illustrated in the example above, is only one of many forms of casual appraisals, which would be entirely unacceptable for most business, and all tax-related contexts. Video tape inventories of your household property and quick "laundry list" appraisals do not fulfill the definition of a "qualified appraisal". Nor do a dealer's offered price to purchase your collection, or the estimates of an auction house.

The dealer's proposed price is not acceptable as a valid appraisal because they have a prospective financial interest in the property that they may be trying to acquire from you. Auction house estimates may - under certain, but not all circumstances - represent a qualified appraised value. Someone who must liquidate property at auction at any price to raise cash may reasonably agree and desire lower estimates in order to attract more spirited bidding. Auction prices may also be subject to rigged bidding or to overpricing when there are two or more bidders who are willing to pay any price to have the winning bid. As a result, auction prices and estimates are only one of several components of an appraisal that affects the valuation.

Adding to the confusion is the fact that any antique or collectible actually has several different values, the three most relevant being: insurance value, fair market value, and marketable cash value. The purpose of an appraisal generally dictates which of these different value definitions is relevant.

An expert, detailed analysis with supporting data will allow you to defend the valuation designated by the appraisal should it become necessary. It is important to note that the IRS will assume a position, in any dispute, that is most favorable to them and not to you. Reasonable people may disagree and, most importantly, remember than any appraisal is as much an art as a science. There are many shades of grey between the black and white areas. However, keep in mind, the general definition of value is the price that a willing buyer

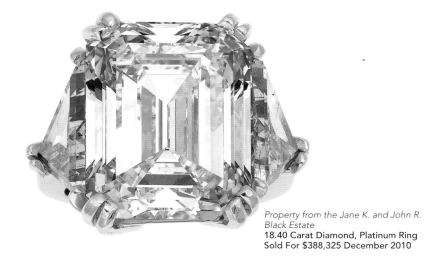

and a willing seller will negotiate with one another, with neither party under any compulsion to buy or sell.

A note about appraisal regulations: There is no single, unified government document or regulation that comprehensively prescribes the appraisal content and processes required for income tax, estate tax, and gift tax purposes. A growing body of government, government-sponsored, and private organizations are coordinating all of their efforts –more or less together- to regulate the appraisal industry and establish unified standards.

The Uniform Standards for Professional Appraisal Practice (USPAP), published by the Congress-authorized Appraisal Foundation, determines the content, qualifications and ethics standards for the appraisal profession.

The Internal Revenue Service, of course, has an assortment of regulatory requirements that are, unfortunately, dispersed throughout the tax code. In practice, guidelines technically written for donation appraisals are often used as guidance for estate appraisals, and vice versa. This is despite the fact that the taxpayer will hope for a higher appraised value when making a charitable donation or transfer to a charitable trust and a lower valuation for estate tax purposes.

Each major appraisal organization has its own written regulations, which members must follow, such as the Appraisers Association of

America's "Elements of a Correctly Prepared Appraisal."

A museum cataloging system known as the Getty Object ID is considered the standard for describing objects in a qualified appraisal, though the IRS has set preferences of how it would like items described in certain $20,000+ appraisals - and also have preferred methods of imaging to be included with appraisals.

Finally, the Pension Protection Act of 2006 and its subsequent guidance radically changed the appraisal profession by legislating higher standards and increasing appraiser penalties.

An appraiser is wise to employ a cumulative approach to the various regulatory requirements of ALL of these authorities in order to assure all bases are covered.

The most common situations in which tangible personal property must be valued for tax purposes are:

- When a taxpayer claims a charitable deduction on his or her income tax return.

- When an executor values a decedent's personal effects.

- When a taxpayer reports the value of a gift on a gift tax return.

Other purposes are discussed in this text, including regulations governing excess benefit transactions that involve certain exempt organizations. In each case the taxpayer or executor may be required to supply or rely upon an appraisal of the property and the specific requirements are different in each situation.

DIFFERENT TYPES OF VALUES AND APPRAISALS

To understand the three most relevant definitions of value, we will use an example of an item that is brought to auction and is sold for a hammer price of $1,000. There is a 20% buyer's premium, $200, added to the cost of $1,000. The purchaser, who is a dealer, tries to sell the item in his store for $2,400. Since the buyer has to pay the premium of $200, his cost is the fair market value of $,1200 representing the $1,000 hammer price plus the buyer's premium of $200. The marketable cash value is $1,000 which represents the actual sale or "hammer" price of the item. The insurance value is $2,400 which is the retail sales price or resale price.

Income Tax and Charitable Donations

Charitable donation appraisals use Fair Market Value (FMV) as the controlling definition of value and the appraisal report is essentially the same as for the estate tax appraisal.

The most complicated of appraisal requirements are those required of a taxpayer claiming a charitable deduction. For any item of tangible personal property valued at more than $5,000, the taxpayer must obtain a "Qualified Appraisal" and attach an "Appraisal Summary" to the income tax return. If any item is valued at more than $20,000, the taxpayer must attach the Qualified Appraisal itself to the tax return rather than only the Summary Appraisal. The appraisal regulations under section 170 specify in detail the requirements of a Qualified Appraisal. These requirements are also summarized in IRS Publication 561, "Determining the Value of Donated Property."

Taxpayers and advisors should keep in mind that this publication is intended only for assistance in preparing income tax returns, and is not applicable for estate or gift tax returns, although many of the concepts are the same or similar.

The four general requirements of a Qualified Appraisal are as follows:

(A) It must be made not more than 60 days before the date of the contribution of the property to the charity and not later than the due date of the return on which a deduction for the contribution is claimed.

(B) No part of the fee for the appraisal can be based on a percentage of the appraised value of the property.

(C) It must be prepared and signed by a "Qualified Appraiser" and all appraisers who contribute to its preparation must also sign it.

(D) It must include:

(1) A detailed description of the property in a form that someone who is not generally familiar with the type of property

would be able to recognize this particular item. For certified coins the description should include the certifying organization, such as PCGS, NGC or ANACS and the certification number on the case;

(2) A description of the physical condition of the property. For certified coins the grade of the coin on the case is sufficient;

(3) The date (or expected date) of contribution;

(4) The terms of any agreement that the donor has entered into or expects to enter with regard to the property;

(5) The name, address and taxpayer ID number of the Qualified Appraiser or Appraisers and if the Qualified Appraiser is employed or engaged as an independent contractor by another person or firm, the name, address and taxpayer ID number of that person or firm;

(6) The qualifications of the Qualified Appraiser who signs the appraisal, including the appraiser's background, experience, education and any membership in professional appraisal associations;

(7) A statement that the appraisal was prepared for income tax purposes;

(8) The date or dates the property was valued;

(9) The appraised fair market value on the date of the contribution;

(10) The method of valuation used to determine the fair market value;

(11) The specific basis for the valuation;

(12) A description of the fee arrangement between the donor and appraiser.

The regulations under section 170 provide very detailed guidelines concerning the qualifications of a Qualified Appraiser. These guidelines are intended to ensure that the Qualified Appraiser is competent to make the appraisal and is sufficiently disinterested to be able to render an honest opinion of value. The regulations provide:

(A) Certain individuals are not allowed to be Qualified Appraisers, including:

    (1) The donor of the property (or taxpayer who claims the deduction);

    (2) The donee of the property;

    (3) A party to the transaction in which the donor acquired the property, such as the person who sold the property to the donor, unless the donor makes the donation within two months of acquiring the property and claims an appraised value no higher than the price at which it was acquired;

    (4) A person who regularly prepares appraisals for one of the above and who does not perform a majority of his or her appraisals for other persons;

    (5) A person employed by or related to any of the above persons in (1), (2) or (3) above.

(B) A Qualified Appraiser must certify on the Appraisal Summary that he or she:

    (1) Holds himself or herself out to the public as an appraiser, or performs appraisals on a regular basis;

    (2) Is qualified to make appraisals of the type of property being valued because of the qualifications in the appraisal;

    (3) Is not one of the excluded individuals named above;

    (4) Is not receiving an appraisal fee based upon a percentage of the appraised property value; and

    (5) Understands that there is a penalty for aiding and abetting under a statement of tax liability.

(C)   A person cannot be a Qualified Appraiser if the donor has knowledge of facts that would cause a reasonable person to expect that the appraiser will overstate the value of the donated property.

A taxpayer who claims a charitable deduction greater than $500 must attach IRS Form 8283 to their income tax return and complete Section A of the form, which requires detailed information about the donated property and the donation. When a taxpayer claims a deduction for an item valued at more than $5,000, he or she must also complete Section B of the form. Section B is the "Appraisal Summary."

The Appraisal Summary requires additional information about the donated property as well as the signature of the donee and a certification signed by the Qualified Appraiser containing the representations described above.

In 1996, the IRS issued Revenue Procedure 96-15, which provides the procedures through which a taxpayer may request from the IRS a binding (on the IRS and the taxpayer) "Statement of Value" as to any item of art that has been appraised at $50,000 or more. The taxpayer may then use the Statement of Value to substantiate the value of the property for income, estate or gift tax purposes.

A taxpayer who requests a Statement of Value from the IRS to substantiate a charitable contribution of property must submit to the IRS a Qualified Appraisal, a required user fee of $2,500 and an Appraisal Summary. Because the taxpayer can request a Statement of Value only after the contribution has been made, the procedures outlined in Revenue Procedure 96-15 may not be of practical use to the taxpayer.

A taxpayer requesting a Statement of Value for estate or gift tax purposes must submit to the IRS an appraisal containing certain specified information, a required user fee of $2,500, a description of the item, the appraised fair value of the item, the cost, date and manner of acquisition and the date of death (or alternate valuation date, if applicable) or the date of the gift. Again, obtaining a Statement of Value is often of little practical use to the taxpayer as it just accelerates the review of values and is therefore of nominal assistance in planning or tax reductions.

Estate Tax Purposes

Unlike Insurance appraisals, the type of value required for estate appraisals is Fair Market Value (FMV), a government defined value construct that is found in approximately 250 different places in the tax code. While the IRS accepts the sale price of liquidated estate assets as the most probative evidence of the property's FMV, unsold estate assets must be appraised according to the FMV definition. For a full discussion of the FMV definition, consult the Trusts & Estates page of the Heritage Web site at www.HA.com/Estates.

Essential to FMV determination for estate purposes is that it is determined effective as of the date of death, of the decedent, or if so elected by the executor, an alternate legal (as opposed to actual) date of death six months later. Fair Market Value does not take into consideration possible future values. This fixed date of effect can be significant in today's fast rising art and collectibles market. Valuation as of the date of death and six months later may vary and affect the tax consequences on the estate. Obviously, you will want to elect the date that provides the lower of the two values to minimize your estate value.

For unsold estate property, appraisers typically determine FMV by applying a market comparative approach. Past sales results of similar items, in a typical marketplace, and within a timely period, are analyzed to suggest the value of the estate item. Fair market value has been defined as the value established where there is a willing buyer and a willing seller, neither of whom is under a compulsion to buy or sell.

For items valued at or above $5,000, appraisal standards require that the appraiser list the comparables that have been used in arriving at a value. The sale venue, date, and location of the comparable's sale should be mentioned, as well as lot numbers and sale numbers in the case of public auctions. As the sale prices of the comparables used may not correspond to that of the determined value of the estate item, a detailed explanation of the relevance of these comparables is also required. Other factors effecting value should also be documented,, such as exhibition history, provenance, and condition issues. Tax court judges have rejected estate appraisers in the past, not for their opinions of value per se, but for failing to explain the reasoning behind them.

For items valued at $20,000 or more, the IRS requires the appraisal report include a good diagnostic photograph of the item. Artworks of this value and higher are also reviewed by the IRS Art Advisory Panel, a committee of art experts from various fields, formed to police underreported valuations.

When an estate includes household and personal effects, the executor must file and complete Schedule F of the estate tax return, itemizing the property and reporting its value. All items of property must be listed separately unless it has a value of less than $100. Items having a value less than $100, and contained in the same room on the date of death, can be grouped together. As an alternative to itemizing, the executor may provide a written statement, prepared under penalties of perjury, setting forth the aggregate value of the property as appraised by competent appraisers of recognized standing and ability (or by dealers in the class of property involved).

As a practical matter, in large estates one or more appraisers value almost all "miscellaneous property." The reasons for this include (1) that the alternative to itemizing, mentioned above, requires that executors rely on appraisals by either a competent appraiser or a dealer, and (2) that the Internal Revenue Code prescribes penalties for both undervaluing and overvaluing estate property. These penalties may be waived on a showing of "reasonable cause and good faith," which may be demonstrated by justifiable reliance on a professional appraisal.

In determining whether reliance on a particular appraisal demonstrated "reasonable cause and good faith," the IRS will take into account: (1) the methodology and assumptions underlying the appraisal, (2) the appraised value, (3) the relationship between appraised value and purchase price, (4) the circumstances under which the appraisal was obtained, and (5) the appraiser's relationship to the taxpayer or to the activity in which the property is used.

Certain types of tangible personal property must be appraised separately; specifically, items having marked artistic or intrinsic value in excess of $3,000, such as jewelry, furs, silverware, paintings, etchings, antiques, books, vases, oriental rugs or coin and stamp collections. The appraisal of such items must be made by an "expert or experts," and it must be made under oath, an often overlooked requirement. The appraisal must also be accompanied by the executor's written statement, made under penalties of perjury, as to the completeness of the itemized list of such property and as to the disinterested character and the qualifications of the appraiser or appraisers.

The regulations provide little guidance regarding the preparation of estate tax appraisals. They merely provide guidance for appraisals of specific types of property:

(1) Books in sets by standard authors should be listed in separate groups;

(2) In listing paintings having artistic value, the size, subject, and artist's name should be stated;

(3) In the case of oriental rugs, the size, make, and general condition should be given; and

(4) In the case of silverware, sets of silverware should be listed in separate groups, groups of individual pieces of silverware should be weighed and the weights given in troy ounces and, in arriving at the value of silverware, the appraisers should take into consideration its antiquity, utility, desirability, condition and obsolescence.

Additional general and specific guidance for estate tax appraisals has been provided in Revenue Procedure 66-49, which suggests that, for general purposes, an appraisal report should contain at least the following:

(1) A summary of the appraiser's qualifications;

(2) A statement of value and the appraiser's definition of the value they obtained;

(3) The basis upon which the appraisal was made; and

(4) The signature of the appraiser and the date the appraisal was made.

Gift Tax Purposes

A taxpayer who makes a completed gift is required to file a gift tax return on IRS Form 709 and, except to the extent of a deduction such as the charitable or marital deduction, pay tax on the transfer at graduated rates based on the value of the gift if the gift generates a tax in excess of the unified credit amount.

As addressed earlier in this book, annual gifts that are within the allowable amount of $13,000 per donor or $26,000 if both spouses participate, the donor, or donors, is not required to file a form or pay a tax. However, when the gifts exceed the annual limits and reduce the lifetime gift tax exemptions, a form must be completed to assist the IRS In the determination of the amount remaining in your exemption, as well as that of your spouse if joint gifts have been made or are contemplated.

The instructions for the gift tax return and the applicable regulations require that the taxpayer attach either a detailed description of the method used to determine the fair market value of the gifted property or an appraisal of the gifted property to the return.

The regulations provide specific guidance regarding the preparation of gift tax appraisals. Although fairly general and applicable to gifts of many types of property, the regulations specify that a gift tax appraisal contain the following information:

(1)   The date of the gift;

(2)   The date on which the gifted property was appraised and the purpose of the appraisal;

(3)   A description of the gifted property;

(4)   A description of the qualifications of the appraiser;

(5)   A description of the appraisal process used;

(6)   Any information considered in determining the appraised value;

(7)   The appraisal procedures followed, and the reason that supports the analyses, opinion and conclusions reached in the appraisal;

(8)   The valuation method used, the rationale for the valuation method, and the procedure used in determining the fair market value of the gifted property; and;

(9)   The specific basis for the valuation, such as specific comparable sales or transactions.

The regulations also specify that an individual must meet the following criteria to prepare a gift tax appraisal:

(1)   Holds themselves out to the public as an appraiser, or performs appraisals on a regular basis;

(2)   Is qualified to make appraisals of the type of property being valued because of their qualifications, as described in the appraisal; and

(3)   Is not the donor or recipient of the property or member of the family of the donor or recipient (which includes spouses, ancestors, lineal descendants and spouses of lineal descendants) or any person employed by the donor, the recipient or a member of the family of either the donor or recipient.

The rules for the appraisal of tangible personal property may seem complicated but can become critically important if the advisor engages an appraiser who is not thoroughly familiar with them. For this reason, an advisor should ensure that the appraiser has up-to-date knowledge of appraisal formats as well as the marketplace in which the most sustainable comparable values can be found.

Insurance Appraisal

Insurance appraisals are indicative of one the three basic definitions of value as we have discussed. Insurance value is also known as Retail Replacement Value (RRV). The intent is to provide a professionally determined basis for making an insured client financially whole in the event of theft, loss or damage as defined by the terms of the insurance policy of the client. It represents a premium value due based on the time involved in locating a replacement in a retail setting, without the element of finding a replacement in an alternate setting, or waiting for the best available replacement.

RRV is generally the highest definition of value taking into account that replacing an item may require such expenses as airfare to a specific destination, a large crating and freight bill and any number of related expenses.

Some Insurance companies "cash out" only at the actual value needed to replace the item. For this reason it is important to determine an accurate and realistic insurance value rather than one that is unreasonably high. In certain situations, overpaying on premiums based upon an over-insured amount will not have any advantage. Depending on the language of your policy, an insurance company may exercise the option to replace the item with another one with similar qualities rather than "cashing out".

It is extremely important that an insurance appraisal report describe the item comprehensively and exhaustively so that an inferior example will not be provided as a replacement. Any extant restoration reports must be attached. Documented distinguishing features, and restoration history also facilitates identification should the insured item be stolen.

Insurance appraisals also require that the location of the item be noted, and any adverse factors related to it must be included. Photographs are required for insurance appraisals, and a valuable component of the appraisal.

You should insure your collection whether you maintain it in a safe-deposit box or at home, and particularly if you exhibit or trade portions of it at shows. Your insurance company will probably require an appraisal prior to granting coverage, but even if it is not required, it is in your best interests to secure one. The premiums will be assessed on your stated value, but should there be a claim and the research indicates that the values were overstated; you will not receive the degree of coverage contemplated in your coverage agreement. Just as with jewels, fine art, or furs, if you over-insure your property, all that you accomplish is making the insurance company wealthier.

An insurance appraisal should be calculated based upon the replacement cost – the price you would have to pay if you went out and replaced the collection buying from dealers or at auction. It should not matter whether you paid $10,000 for the collection or $200,000; if it would cost $100,000 to replace it today that is the exact amount that it should be insured for. The pertinent point is that this is a retail appraisal, probably the only appraisal that is most beneficial to the owner. You should be completely certain and satisfied that the appraiser understands that the purpose is for insurance, as most appraisals are for liquidation value.

Premiums may vary by company, but by far, the cheapest coverage is in force when your collection always remains inside a safe-deposit box. This may seem unnecessary, but in the 1980s, a substantial collection of a friend was stolen from his safe-deposit box when a large bank in Boston was vandalized over the weekend. Rare, but it happens.

Another client's bank vault was flooded for five entire days. Estimate that it will cost you one-half percent of the value of the collection for annual safe-deposit box coverage ($500 for $100,000) and at least double that amount if you require coverage outside the bank. Special circumstances may require additional premiums, so read the policy language carefully for exceptions and ask any questions you believe are necessary for you to fully understand the policy.

The reputation of the insurance company is also very, very important. There are certain insurance companies that will strongly dispute each and every claim made by a client, and some are very slow to pay a claim, while other carriers are reasonable and will not dispute a valid claim

Appraisal For Divorce

If you are in the process of seeking a divorce, and a collection is among the marital assets, you will probably be required to obtain an appraisal.

Finances permitting, one party may want to keep the collection rather than have it sold and the proceeds divided between the parties. This could create one more conflict during the divorce. The spouse that would like to maintain the collection will solicit a low appraisal, while the opposing spouse, who wishes to sell, will look for a higher appraisal.

The most equitable resolution to obtain a divorce appraisal is to show the collection to two or three reputable dealers (three is optimal, but may be unnecessary and expensive if the first two are within

20% of each other). Explain to each dealer that you need a written appraisal of the amount that they would pay to purchase the collection outright. Expect the appraiser to have a completed appraisal available within a week or so depending on the complexity of the appraisal.

Assuming that the collection will not be divided, a "one figure" appraisal (e.g. the sum total offer is $20,000) should be sufficient versus pages of individual offers that would increase the appraisal cost unnecessarily.

The most common issue is where one party is interested in the residence or other assets and the other party has an interest in a work of art or a collectible. How should the assets be valued and the property divided among the parties?

Selecting an Appraiser

Selecting the appraiser is the most important part of this process. In addition to the qualifications mentioned earlier, you are searching for an expert who will represent your best interests in providing a knowledgeable and honest evaluation of your collection. Further, the evaluation should match the needs of the situation being addressed. That said, you still need to retain the responsibility of protecting your own interests.

If your collection is comprised of coins, your appraiser should be a life member of the American Numismatic Association (ANA), a member of the Professional Numismatists Guild (PNG), be established for at least five years (and preferably 10) in the same area, have financial references from a reliable bank and have a solid reputation among knowledgeable collectors. This is the ideal. Depending on your location and the relative value of your collection, you may choose to settle for less, but these are the qualifications you should be seeking. If you have a significant collection, it is probably in your best interests to incur higher expenses (if necessary) to engage an appraiser at this level. Remember, such expenses are usually deductible.

Appraisers may be located in private practice, galleries, auction houses, or many other professions. What is crucial is to select an appraiser who has expertise in their field and that has special expertise in a specific area, if necessary. The appraiser should have up-to-date knowledge of the current market place, appraisal practice experience, and knowledge and compliance with USPAP and ethical standards. They cannot have any financial interest whatsoever in the property that is the subject of their appraisal.

For highly valued estates or large charitable donations, where IRS scrutiny is to be anticipated, selecting the appropriate "qualified appraiser" will be of importance in resolving or eliminating any disputes that may arise at a later date. Be certain to request a resume from the prospective appraiser and review It carefully. Where are their backgrounds, certifications, education and work experience? Ask them specifically if they conform to USPAP standards.

What Will it Cost?

A formal appraisal can be an expensive undertaking, but the important considerations are that it is performed properly and accurately and in conformance with the appropriate standards and that the expense is appropriate relative to the value of the collection.

Expect to pay $200 an hour on average. An appraiser in a small town may charge $100-$175 per hour, while appraisers in larger cities or "high rent" districts tend to charge $300-$500 per hour, so $200 is a good average. If the collection is significant, and the material is rare or esoteric - or if the situation is complex or unusually contentious - you may need the services of a top-rate professional. Their rates can rival that of a law firm's fees of $500 plus per hour. We would emphasize, however, that such a level of expertise is usually not necessary for most collections.

In qualifying an appraiser, ask for an approximate charge after discussing the scope and purpose of the appraisal. If the appraiser won't commit to an exact cost and time estimate ("Two to three hours, no more than three," for example), find someone who will. Remember, a "one price," liquidation appraisal will require much less time (and expense) than a line by line, individually-bid "grocery list."

There may be no costs involved in certain circumstances. Some dealers will provide you with a dated, written offer to purchase your collectibles on a no-obligation basis. Unless you require insurance appraisal values, that offer will be acceptable as a liquidation appraisal. Others dealers may charge you for a written appraisal with the caveat that if you sell them the collection by an arbitrary date, the appraisal fees will be rebated. Dealers would much rather purchase collections than appraise them and you can use that leverage to your advantage. In all fairness, however, if someone does a "free" appraisal," you should at least allow them the opportunity to bid when you make a decision to sell.

You May Not Need an Appraisal Report

If you are not filing a tax return, donating non-cash assets to a non-profit or obtaining insurance for your collectibles, you may not need a qualified appraisal report. The expense and time required to develop a formal appraisal may be avoided in certain circumstances. Many uninformed people mistakenly seek an "appraisal" when only general guidance as to value is required.

If your objective is to sell your collection, and you are interested in determining the amount a dealer would pay for your collection, most dealers will be pleased to make an offer or provide you with their best estimate of value without the labor and expense of creating a formal appraisal report. Similarly, an auction house will usually provide you with their auction estimates free of charge based upon the possibility of its being selected to auction the contents of your collection.

There may also be private appraisers who will inspect and provide you with a verbal appraisal of the property at a reduced rate.

Safety of Collectibles During Appraisal

It is your responsibility to ensure the safety of your collection during the appraisal. You should expect it to cost more, but once you have selected an appraiser, the safest method is to have the appraiser meet with you at the bank. A true professional will generate an inventory if one does not already exist and then make evaluation notes in the safe-deposit room. The appraiser will then take the notes back to their office to determine values and draft the appraisal. Explain the timeframe to the appraiser and don't forget to request an estimate for their time. Even a modest collection, appraised under these ideal conditions (ideal for you, but NOT necessarily for the dealer) will probably be charged at several hours.

A less expensive alternative is to transport the collectibles to the dealer and remain with them when the appraisal notes are being made. You can then return at an agreed upon date to procure the appraisal. If your location or schedule requires you to either ship or leave your collection for appraisal, you should put more effort into qualifying your appraiser. This is simply good business and a natural step in assuring the safety of your collection.

In summary: Determine the scope of your collection, and what you are attempting to accomplish with an appraisal. Select the professional who combines the qualifications and economies best suited to your situation, and safeguard your collection during the process.

What is a Qualified Appraiser?

IRS regulation 170(f)(11)(E)(ii) provides that the term "qualified appraiser" is defined as an individual, who (1) has earned an appraisal designation from a recognized professional appraiser organization, or has otherwise met minimum education and experience requirements set forth in regulations prescribed by the Secretary, (2) regularly performs appraisals for which the individual receives compensation, and (3) meets other such requirements as may be prescribed by the Secretary in regulations or other guidance.

Section 170(f)(11)(E)(iii) provides that an individual will not be treated as a qualified appraiser unless that individual (1) demonstrates verifiable education and experience in valuing the type of property subject to the appraisal, and (2) has not been prohibited from practicing before the IRS by the Secretary under Sec. 330(c) of Title 31 of the United States Code at any time during the 3-year period ending on the date of the appraisal.

The Appraisal Report

To meet all the current professional standards, an appraisal report prepared for any purpose will typically contain a substantial amount of prescribed information, among which is:

The property owner's name and address

The name, contact information, tax payer ID and qualifications of the appraiser

The purpose of the appraisal

The valuation approach employed

The value definition used

A marketplace analysis

Date of inspection

Cost, date and manner of acquisition of the subject property, if known

Current opinion of value

Effective date of the appraisal

Date of document

A detailed catalog description of each item following the Getty Object ID format

Supporting evidence (comparable past sales data)

A host of other formal and content requirements, even including pagination style.

USPAP requires that an appraisal report of tangible property must include a Certification Statement from the appraiser which states:

The statements of fact contained in this report are true and correct

The reported analyses, opinions and conclusions are limited only by the reported assumptions and limiting conditions and are my personal, impartial, and unbiased professional analyses, opinions and conclusions

I have no (or specified) present or prospective interest in the property that is the subject of this report, and no (or specified) personal interest with respect to the parties involved

I have no bias with respect to the property that is the subject of this report or to the parties involved in the assignment

My engagement in this assignment was not contingent upon developing or reporting predetermined results

My compensation for completing this assignment is not contingent upon the development or reporting of a predetermined value or direction in value that favors the cause of the client, the amount of the value opinion, the attainment of a stipulated result, or the occurrence of a subsequent event directly related to the intended use of this appraisal

My analyses, opinions and conclusions were developed, and this report has been prepared, in conformity of the Uniform Standards for Professional Appraisal Practice

I have (or have not) made a personal inspection of the property that is the subject of this report. (If more than one person signs this Certification, the Certification must clearly specify which individuals did and which individuals did not make a personal inspection of the appraised property

No one provided significant personal property appraisal assistance to the person signing this certification. (If there are exceptions, the name of each individual providing significant personal property appraisal assistance must be stated here.)

Subsequent guidance, Notice 2006-96, relating to the appraisal standard changes in the Pension Protection Act of 2006 also requires the appraiser to certify that:

The appraiser understands that a substantial or gross valuation misstatement resulting from an appraisal of the value of the property that the appraiser knows, or reasonably should have known, would be used with a return or claim for refund, may subject the appraiser to civil penalty under Sec. 6695A. (emphasize, "civil penalty").

Clearly, the days of the cursory "laundry list" appraisal are over. Historically unregulated, appraisers of tangible property are now mandated to meet higher USPAP and IRS standards. In the USPAP regulations is a Competency Rule, requiring an appraiser to possess both the knowledge and experience necessary to perform any assignment undertaken, or to take the necessary steps to acquire this competency through study or association with other appraisers. Several new laws concerning appraisal standards, including increased appraiser penalties, were also ratified as part of the Pension Protection Act of 2006.

There are also increased restrictions on who is considered to be a qualified appraiser for donation appraisals. The appraiser cannot be related to or associated with either the donor or the donee.

Appraisals of Collectibles – In General

IRS publication 561 includes specific guidelines regarding the appraisal of collections and coins as well as other collectibles. The following is a summary of the appropriate standards recommended by the IRS for appraising coins and collectibles which are contained in IRS Publication 561, "Determining the Value of Donated Property".

This publication indicates that many of the factors that are significant in the appraisal of art objects apply also to collectibles and we will include those standards in our analysis of the factors involved in the appraisal of coins and other collectibles.

First, the authenticity of the item or object must be determined by the appraiser.

One of the components in the appraisal process related to the physical condition of the object and the extent of any restoration that has been performed on the item. These have a significant effect on the value and must be fully reported in an appraisal.

It is important to select the appropriate appraiser. More weight will usually be afforded to an appraisal prepared by an individual specializing in the kind and price range of the art being appraised. Certain dealers are specialists in their respective fields. Their opinions on the authenticity and desirability of such objects are given more weight than the opinions of more generalized appraisers. They can report more recent comparable sales to support their opinions.

Publications available to help you determine the value of many kinds of collections include catalogs, dealers' price lists and specialized hobby periodicals. When using one of these price guides, you must use the current edition at the date of contribution. However these sources are not always reliable indicators of FMV and should be supported by other evidence. The price that an item may have sold for in an auction may have been the result of a rigged sale or a mere bidding duel. The appraiser must analyze the reference material, and recognize and make adjustments for misleading entries.

Publication 561 specifically refers to coin collections. Many catalogs and other reference materials show the writer's or publisher's opinion of the value of coins on or near the date of the publication. Like many other collector items, the value of a coin depends on demand, age and rarity. Another important factor is the coin's condition. For example, there is a great difference in the value of a coin that is in mint condition and a similar coin that is only in good condition.

Catalogs usually establish a category for coins based on their physical condition - mint or uncirculated extremely fine, very fine, fine very good, good, fair, or poor - with a different valuation for each category.

A few facts for those who collect other objects of art.

Some tips for book collectors: The value of books is usually determined by selecting comparable sales and adjusting the prices according to the differences between the comparable sales and the items being evaluated. This is extremely difficult to accomplish and should be performed by a specialized appraiser. Within the general category of literary property, there are dealers who specialize in certain areas, such as American, foreign imports, Bibles and scientific books.

A book that is very old, or very rare, is not necessarily valuable. There are many books that are very old, or rare, but that have little or no market value. The condition of a book may have a great influence on its value. Collectors are interested in items that are in fine, or at least good, condition. When a book has a missing page, loose binding, tears, stains, or is otherwise in poor condition its value is greatly diminished.

Other factors used in the valuation of books are the kind of binding (leather, cloth, paper) page edges, and illustrations (drawings and photographs). Collectors usually want first editions of books. However, because of changes or additions, other editions are sometimes worth as much as, or more than, the first edition.

What about the stamp collectors? Valuations are primarily based on the standard catalogs available (Scott and others). Condition, supply and demand, liquidity, rarity and beauty apply to the valuation of stamps, as well as other collectibles. Generally, two prices are indicated for each stamp: the price postmarked and the price not postmarked. Stamp dealers generally know the value of their merchandise and are able to prepare satisfactory appraisals of valuable collections.

There are many collectors of manuscripts, autographs, diaries, and similar items. When these items are handwritten, or at least signed by famous people, they are often in great demand and are valuable. The writings of unknowns also may be of value if they are of unusual historical importance. Determining the value of such material is very difficult.

For example, there may be a great difference in value between two diaries that were kept by a famous person - one kept during childhood and the other during a later period in their life. The appraiser determines a value in these situations by applying knowledge and judgment to such factors as comparable sales and conditions.

Signatures, or sets of signatures that were removed from letters or other papers, usually have little or no value. Complete sets of the signatures of U.S. presidents, however, are in great demand.

Knowledge is power. Although, you may not be the appraiser, this information will assist you in understanding the steps that are important to an appraisal and will allow you to ask the right questions of the appraiser.

If you do not believe that the IRS is interested in appraisal methodology, these last several paragraphs are taken directly from IRS publication 561.

TIPS FOR HEIRS: If you have created a basic inventory where none existed previously, request a "ball park" estimate of the value of the collection in your initial discussions with potential appraisers. Because the condition of any collectible is such an important issue, they may be reluctant. They should, however, be able to explain to you whether or not you are dealing with a collection that is of substantial value or not. That information should help you calculate the expenses related to the process.

At that stage of the process, we recommend that you expend additional time and energy to properly qualify an appraiser, especially if you are not a collector and are unfamiliar with the "players" in the marketplace. Be prepared before you start meeting with prospective appraisers. Often, individuals who request formal appraisals appear to create an adversarial relationship with the appraiser. This may be a result of an often mistaken belief that the owner knows the true value of the subject of the appraisal.

This strange dynamic often inhibits owners from disclosing relevant information to the appraiser. It might involve some previous damage to the property that has now been expertly repaired and is invisible to the naked eye. Or it may be related to the facts and circumstances related to the acquisition of the item. Regardless of their motivation, owners have an ethical and moral obligation to inform and disclose to their appraisers all of the relevant facts in order for the appraiser to make informed judgments that will withstand further scrutiny.

The obligation may be contractual if the Appraisal Agreement includes language requiring the owner to disclose any and all information known or documented regarding the subject property. Failure to provide this information, including any old invoices, auction records and past appraisal reports, may void the appraisal agreement and release the appraiser from any liability resulting from omissions or failure to fully disclose relevant information. An appraiser cannot accept any information provided to them as a matter of fact without independent confirmation.

When the appraiser arrives, show them your updated written inventory document, with all of the supporting documentation and allow them to add value opinions to it. They will probably need to physically inspect all of the items and create their own, notarized appraisal document. Preparation will save you time and money. Heritage Auctions Appraisal Services (HA.com/ appraise) can work with you on the proper form of the appraisal to meet necessary purposes, the associated costs of producing the appraisal and the timeline of completion of the final appraisal document.

PART FOUR

Disposing Of Your Collection

10

Selling Your Collection Through Outright Sale

This chapter is the first of three that outline specific methods for disposing of your collection. Each has benefits for certain types of collectibles, and is weaker when it comes to others. The common thread is that each method subscribes to the philosophy that "time is money."

This means that, all other things being equal, the sooner that you receive payment for your collection, the less money you are likely to receive. This is not necessarily an unfair situation, as you will see in these chapters. We are going to try to place you inside the minds of your potential purchasers, and assist you in understanding their motives for buying your collection. Their time is valuable, as is yours. Our goal is to aid you in making a measured decision about the amount of time you are willing to invest in the disposition process.

Outright sale is without question the easiest method of selling a whole or partial collection. You present the articles to one or more buyers. They make offers. You either accept or decline. The time you are investing in this process is limited to the period you are present with the collectibles at the evaluation(s); if you accept an offer, you receive your payment and go on with your life. If you assembled the collection this can be devastating or it can be cathartic, but it won't take forever.

First, we will assume that you are offering a collection of substance to a dealer within your specific collectible type. Dealers are most likely to have both the motivation and wherewithal to buy an entire collection. It is also easier to locate them through their advertising and they can be qualified through their references and affiliations. What is the dealer thinking when you bring him your collection to bid?

Dealers are in business to buy collections coming through the front door (or through the mail). Most of their advertising and their longevity at a particular site are planned specifically to induce such an environment. Many collectibles are a fixed-supply commodity. If you're in the business, you have to acquire products to sell, and advantageous buying is at the core of such a business. The dealer wants to purchase your collection – it's their raison d'être – and the nicer the collection, the more they want it.

We have two parties together; one who wants to sell and one who wants to buy. Now comes the sticking point. In any trading situation, the final result reflects the combination of knowledge and leverage of the parties. The dealer wants to buy the collection at the lowest price they can pay without it walking out the door. Their leverage is that they have the money and willingness to acquire the entire collection, plus any degree of impatience that you possess, or they can instill in you. You may also believe that they are more knowledgeable about current markets than you are as a result of their experience and credentials. You, however, want to know that you are receiving the maximum reasonable price for your collectibles. Your leverage is that they do not want to let you out the door with the collection. Your knowledge and negotiating skills are also an advantage.

A dealer is bidding on three separate planes when a collection is offered to them. First, there are those items for which they know they have customers, or which are readily liquid in their retail or "high wholesale" operations. These will generally be priced well because their risk and expense of holding inventory is minimal.

Second, are the articles that do not fit that criteria: collectibles that are not routinely traded and which will require greater effort to sell. This particularly applies to bulk, where additional shipping weight is also a factor. Such items will be figured cheaply because of the effort and expense necessary to resell them at a profit. This may seem callous, but it's a matter of perspective. Some of your collectibles may be very special to you, but those same pieces sitting unsold on a dealer's shelf are merely inventory that is incurring additional interest. They will take the time to find the "high buyer" because that is how they makes a living, but their bid for those items will reflect both their intent to make a profit at the wholesale level, and will reflect any uncertainty about the high buyer and their buying levels.

The third factor is not related to the collectibles, but rather the dealer's perception of their competition. If you live in a small town with only one dealer (in the field of your collectible), their basic assumption may be that they pretty much own the market. This may also apply in any location where the dealer perceives that you are not "shopping." Their bid will not be competitive.

There are those who will read the last paragraph and mumble about "rip-off" dealers, but the reality is endemic throughout society and business in general, not just this portion of it; it lies at the very heart of Capitalism. Americans as a whole are not taught to function in a barter system or to become natural negotiators. We go to the store and buy what we want at the marked price, only sometimes, perhaps, after checking the newspapers for sales. It's what we have learned in childhood and by the time we are adults; most of us are conditioned to the process. As a result, a large percentage of people still pay "sticker price" even in environments where some negotiating is expected.

When selling or trading something in, the same conditioning applies – the dealer establishes the market and, as the perceived authority figure, a surprisingly large number of people accept that quote as fact - or at least believe that their only options are "yes" or "no." The dealer, of course, falls into that group of people who, through aptitude or training, are both comfortable and experienced in negotiating (that is, appearing not to be negotiating). Naturally, you need to use your collection and your business skills in their best light if you want to receive a better price for your collectibles, whatever they are.

Here are some tips for negotiating the best deal on your collection:

• Know the Best Items for Direct Sale
To obtain the best prices from direct sale, consider all of the following tips and how you might apply them to your effort.

• Allow yourself a National Marketplace
The world has become a much smaller place through increasingly rapid communications and transportation as well as due to widespread Internet use. You should not limit your search for outlets to your hometown. If your collection is significant and of substantial value, the outlets will come to you!

• Find a "Full Service" Dealer

Remember the earlier remarks about liquidity-based bidding. A large dealer with a wide clientele and business contacts will "see" your more common items as more liquid because they routinely sell this kind of material as well as the "good" collectibles. They already know who the high buyers are and what they're paying. Additionally, because of their business volume, they will not have the need (or temptation) to "make their month" on your collection. As a result, they're more likely to bid the whole deal "closer."

• Create an "Aura of Competition"

It is rarely a bad idea to obtain more than one bid on something you are selling and never a bad idea to let a potential buyer know that other people are bidding (whether they are or not). This can be communicated after you get a bid – "Is this your best offer, Mr. Smith? I know dealers sometimes leave a little 'wiggle room,' but I have two other people bidding and this isn't that kind of negotiation" – or before – "I want you to know in advance, Mr. Smith, that I'm offering the collection for bid to three people. Please give me your best offer the first time."

• Display Your Knowledge in Discussing the Bid

Dealers and people handling collectibles respect those who speak the language. You don't necessarily have to have a deep knowledge if you can "sell" yourself on a few key points. If you have a few pieces in your collection that stand out, bring them up. "What do you bid for this, Mr. Smith?" Similarly, you should get a feel for the levels being offered for your second tier material.

• "Play the Player"

You needn't be a market expert to get the "feel" of a collection if you are at all adept at reading others. Follow up the responses to the questions above with further questions. "You bid ____? Isn't that a little low?" If the dealer can immediately address the questions with logic and weigh options, he may be extremely glib, but more likely he is comfortable with his offer. Alternatively, if he's evasive or there's no logic to his response, there's very likely negotiating room left in the offer.

• Split the Deal

Rather than offer the whole collection in one lot, offer "test" groups for bid to get a feel for your potential buyers. Generally, there is more control when dealing with smaller, manageable "pieces" and you can often secure more money. There is also the "bait" technique of letting the bidders know that there is more beyond. This perception may lead some bidders to treat you better in the early rounds. The trade-off is more of your time.

In summary, only you can decide how much of your time you are prepared to invest in the disposition of your collection. Generally, the more productive time that is devoted to the endeavor, the better the result. You can be most effective in preparing for disposition by knowing your collection, knowing the market and knowing your potential buyers.

TIPS FOR HEIRS: If you are a non-collector and after reading this chapter you want to use this method, we would recommend strongly that you seek multiple offers. We would also recommend that you first read and consider the options that are discussed in the next two chapters as well.

Patek Philippe Ref. 5036/1J-001
Men's Gold Moonphase Annual
Calendar Wristwatch with Power
Reserve Indicator, circa 2002
Sold for: $21,510, May 2009

11

Selling Your Collectibles Through an Agent

"Sales are contingent upon the attitude of the salesman –
not the attitude of the prospect." -W. Clement Stone

It may be practical for you or your heirs to use the services of an agent to sell your collection. The objective in choosing this method is to receive more money than you would receive from a direct sale. The trade-off (again) is that it will take more time and effort. That said, you might even wish to enlist the services of several agents to sell different parts of your collection.

Many people employ an agent to assist them in selling real estate. The agent knows real estate values, has methods to contact qualified customers, and understands how to negotiate with them. A good dealer has the same qualifications and contacts in their field, but you rarely hear the term "agent" used in that context. Dealers would generally prefer to purchase collections outright (at the lower price), and then have the freedom to resell them without customer consultation. They may, however, accept a collection on consignment rather than allow it to walk out the door.

A client/agent relationship is a relatively long one. As the owner of multiple properties may commission the real estate agent to dispose of one at a time, so may the owner of a collection turn over its elements in groups. This allows the agent to focus more narrowly and allows you to maintain control. The key is regular communication and interaction between you and the agent. Items that the agent has been given may not sell and must be returned. The asking price may need to be adjusted downward. There may be a change in market conditions. While the agent may be doing most of the work, you, the seller, will need to remain involved. As real estate agents and sellers work together as partners to their mutual benefit, so should you and your agent. The agent should be expected to inform you of market conditions and help in determining prices. Above all, you must be able to trust the agent; to have faith in their ability; and be confident that they are looking after your best interests. One way to gauge this is to test the agent's overall performance with a few collectibles prior to making any major commitment.

An agent is not worth the trouble unless they can get 10% to 25% more than you would receive in a direct sale. Remember, the agent's role is not just to know the collectibles, but also the markets and the players.

The first step in seeking an agent is to determine the nature of what you plan to sell and try to match the right agent with the right product. This may seem obvious, but a common mistake among sellers is to retain unqualified agents. If your pieces are specialized, seek a specialist. If they are mainstream, look for the following kinds of qualifications:

• Scope of Company

The agent (or their company) routinely handles articles of the same type, condition and values as those in your collection, and has strong customer demand for them.

• Grading Service Experience

In the case of coins, the agent (or their company) regularly submits coins to the grading services and has a strong feeling for where the "standard lines" of the grades are. Ideally, the agent or other personnel in their company will have worked for a grading service and understand both the process and "looks" (eye appeal) that are most often rewarded on marginal decisions.

• Regular Show Attendance

The agent (or their company) attends shows on a regular basis where routine contact with other collectors and dealers provides a feel for the market and provides a wide range of business contacts. Taken a step further, attendance at national shows will afford even more insights and opportunity.

• Mailing List

The agent (or their company) has an extensive mailing list and will present your collection to the maximum number of potential buyers.

These qualifications promise the potential of significantly higher returns, but you also want to choose an agent who genuinely seeks the role. Many dealers only want to buy and sell collectibles, and really don't have the time or inclination to assist you as an agent. You should not be distressed if someone that you approach turns you down; you don't want to enlist a reluctant ally. The last thing you need is a dealer who thinks they are doing you a favor by selling your collection.

Many variables can influence the arrangement you make with an agent; however, five important elements should be negotiated in any event:

– The agent's fees should be discussed and agreed upon in advance. Generally, they should receive a percentage of the selling price. This fee is usually graduated and predicated on the value of the collectibles. You cannot expect an agent to go to the trouble and expense of selling a $100 item for a 5% commission. A more equitable arrangement might be a 15% commission on pieces valued under $1,000 and 10% on articles valued over that amount. That, of course, is a matter of negotiation.

A firm minimum price for each item or group of items to be sold should be agreed upon in advance with the understanding that the seller be advised before any articles are sold for less than this fixed price. Relinquishing your collection to an agent in exchange for a promise to do their best is not acceptable. It should be expected that the agent do some research and make a few phone calls prior to suggesting a minimum price. Agents should be prepared to substantiate the values they suggest. Conversely, you should not demand unreasonable minimums. No agent is going to waste their time and energy trying to sell articles that are obviously overpriced.

Negotiating the minimums is a critical component of this kind of arrangement. If you are not comfortable with the value range of your individual collectibles, it may be best to get a written offer first. Then you'll know what you're trying to improve upon before negotiating with an agent.

The agent should be given the exclusive right to sell the collection for a specific period of time. Depending on the nature of the collection, the agent may have standard practices they wish to follow. Allowing the agent a set length of time to sell the collection should be separated from the payment schedule. Within reason, the owner should be paid as the items are sold. A good method to use is to make periodic settlements based on time or dollar amount. If the agent is given 90 days to sell the collection, it would seem fair to request that the agent makes payments at 30 and 60 day intervals, or when the amount collected reaches $5,000 or more. We would be wary of an agent who didn't agree to this proposal. Requesting periodic payments is also a simple and positive way to measure the agent's performance.

- The agent must agree to be totally responsible for the collection while it is in their possession. The agent you select may be the most honorable person on earth, but they would still not be immune to theft or natural disaster. Proof of sufficient insurance coverage is mandatory. In many cases, the most prudent strategy would be to give the agent a limited number of your collectibles to sell at any one time.

- Have the agreement in writing. Good contracts make good trading partners, and this is a business arrangement between two parties. All terms must be spelled out and the document signed by both parties in whatever manner creates a binding contract in your state.

One other area where agents can be useful is in moving "bulk" coins. Bulk is the bane of most coin dealers' existences. Some coin collectors have accumulated 10 proof and mint sets a year for 40 years and can't understand why the dealer is not enthused when three wheel barrows full of coin sets roll through the door. The answers are: low price and low margin plus high (relative) weight. We can virtually guarantee you that if you have an abundance of this material in your collection, it will generally be bid very low as part of any outright purchase offer - probably 70% to 85% of "sheet." From the dealer's perspective, it is cumbersome, difficult to process and likely to sit gathering dust while more lucrative sales of products are prioritized.

Nonetheless, there are a few dealers who specialize in the sale of this kind of material and are the "high buyers." Your agent for this kind of material should know who those high buyers are and be willing to manage the administrative functions of arranging and completing the transactions. In return, they should either receive a mutually agreed fixed fee, perhaps 5%-10%, and expenses. You should still come out ahead of the typical direct sale offer.

In summary, match the agent with the material, establish realistic minimums that make using this method worthwhile, qualify the agent, put the agreement in writing and communicate regularly with the agent throughout the agreement period.

TIPS FOR HEIRS: If you are a non-collector and wish to use this option, we recommend that you obtain an outright purchase offer first. Use extra diligence in qualifying potential agents, and pay close attention to having the agent(s) validate the established minimum prices. Use the direct offers as a comparison and make sure that the minimums offer a significant increase. It may be even more important to offer small test groups to become more comfortable with the process and the agent.

John F. Kennedy: Perhaps the Only Existing Kennedy Rocking Chair with Ironclad Authentication from the Kennedy Family!
Sold For: $65,725 November 2010

12

Selling Your Collection at Auction

"A fair price is the highest one a collector can be induced to pay." – Robert Hughes

The ideal situation for selling any product is to show it to as many potential customers as possible. When the product is rare, competing customers are important, and an auction is frequently the best venue. There are many benefits to this method of disposition, but the primary one is that in a good auction (one with many bidders), each item should realize at least its true worth.

An auction is a truly free market, one where each article stands on its own merits. Every item is examined carefully by those people most interested in it and those willing to back their opinions with money. If you have a collectible that is rare enough that it trades infrequently, its current value would have to be described as uncertain. In an outright purchase of such an item, most dealers will factor that uncertainty into their price unless they absolutely know they have a buyer at a certain level. A well-advertised sale by an established auction house, on the other hand, will likely draw the attention of all the known buyers—and any others as well. The collector community is generally a small one, and most serious buyers are aware when objects of interest are offered for sale, particularly at auction. When that condition exists, competitive demand will dictate the strongest result and produce the truest value for a particular collectible.

Another competitive bidding factor is eye-appeal. All collectibles were not created equal and many people will pay a premium for pieces they consider superior.

Finally, if you have something esoteric – an item that is not traded routinely– a good auction may again bring the very best price. If you have substantial holdings of such, choose an auctioneer with a strong track record for the particular genre – one who has the clientele (both mailing list and attendance) and auction locations to put the collection in front of the greatest number of potential buyers.

These factors are what make an auction the best venue for a wide spectrum of collectibles. Your task is to pick the auctioneer that can put your pieces in front of the right people, preferably in quantity.

When looking for an auctioneer, you should consider the following qualifications:

- **Financial Resources and Stability**
  An auction consignment is first and foremost a business deal. As with contracting an agent, an auctioneer must demonstrate sufficient financial resources to ensure your comfort that they can both effectuate a sale and pay you at the stated settlement date. They must also accept liability and provide full insurance against the loss or damage of your collection.

- **Longevity in the Business**
  The auction is a multi-faceted business operation that requires a great deal of development to assure everything flows smoothly: consignor and bidder bases, cataloging references and expertise, site setup and physical security, auction flow and administrative efficiency – and that only begins to touch on what goes into it. Go with a proven entity; it's your money that's involved.

- **Advertising Resources**
  Success breeds success. You can't have the top sales without great advertising and vice versa. Look for the companies who are doing the major advertising in the trade papers and on the Internet. They stage the sales that justify the cost of full-page ads. The bigger the sale, the more buyers to bid on your collectibles.

- **Location**
  A company that is limited to holding auctions in locations out of the mainstream does not have the ability to attract a large bidder base. Some companies hold auctions in major financial centers with good regional access, while others appropriately utilize the broad reach of the Internet.

- **Competitive Rates**
  Auction companies charge both buyer's and seller's fees to absorb the expenses of the sale and turn a profit. A seller's fee of 15-20% has become the standard and you should not have to pay more, unless your collection has extraordinary "bulk" or requires out-of-the-ordinary attention. Indeed, if you have a significant collection, you may be able to negotiate a better rate.

- **Strong Writing and Imagery**
  Catalog descriptions and photography create the necessary excitement and demand for an auction's collectibles and provide all that is available to entice bidders who cannot attend the sale in person. Our company, Heritage Galleries, is a pioneer in the use of DVDs and the Internet as alternative cataloging media. It's clear that this is the wave of the future. Until that transition has fully occurred, strive for examples of good catalog writing and high quality photography.

- **Professional Personnel**
  It takes quality personnel - and many of them - to conduct a great auction. The auction process is a complex one when done right. Consignment coordination, grading advice, cataloging, customer relations are all important factors.

In qualifying auctioneers, be certain to inquire as to the number of people that will be involved in managing your consignment and what their roles are. Our company provides potential consignors with a video that details the auction process from start to finish, and other companies should at least have literature that covers the same ground. Any company is only as good as its people. Contact a number of reputable auction houses to get an impression as to how they will treat your collection.

Auction is often the best venue for high-quality collectibles, particularly if the items trade infrequently. A good auction attracts the right mix of bidders to establish the real value for each individual piece, often far in excess of the average price.

If this seems the best route for you, interview potential auctioneers to determine which of them combines the best business resources, venues and personnel assets.

As an aside: Our company has expanded its scope of venues to include several kinds of Internet auctions. The Internet is an amazing communications tool that, among other things, allows individuals to perform functions that previously were available only to businesses. Someone asked, "What if a collector or heir wants to sell a collection by themselves on the Internet?" Many auction Web sites - such as eBay, Yahoo and Amazon - are certainly available for just such a project. The question is whether the choice is a good one relative to the other options.

We have a good idea of the basics, so consider the following questions:

— Do you already have a "feedback" rating that will give you credibility with the bidder base? Many Internet auction bidders are concerned or fearful about transactions with strangers. They are, after all, sending their hard-earned money to someone they've never met and probably never heard of. The equalizer is the feedback system that each Internet auction employs to establish "cyber-reputations." In most cases, each party to a "trade" gets the forum to comment on how the other trader performed. Every positive and negative comment is there for future potential traders to evaluate. If you don't have a feedback rating, some bidders will avoid your auctions altogether and others will bid less (as if ameliorating their risk).

— Do you have the equipment and skill to create digital images of the articles to be auctioned? It is a proven fact that Internet auction items that don't have pictures bring much less money. Disregarding the skills, you will need either a high-resolution digital camera or a flatbed scanner, and an image management program to acquire the images. You will also need a Web site, or to learn how to use one of the "free posting" sites to upload your images.

— Do you have the skills to write descriptions for each item? Auction bidders are best motivated when a "story" is available to make the collectible more interesting. It's called "building value," and the visual image and description pro-

Emerald, Diamond, White
Gold Pendant
Sold For: $10,157 May 2010

vide the combination that maximizes an Internet auction's results.

– Do you have the business skills to analyze potential problem situations? Can you collect a bad check or determine whether a "special request" from a customer is legitimate or a scam? Most of the people on the Internet are honest, but there are exceptions. Unfortunately, it doesn't take many bad deals to turn a profitable situation into a loss.

– Do you have the knowledge and resources to ship high-dollar packages to a hundred different people? There is a lot of administrative responsibility in conducting one's own auctions, not the least of which is delivering the goods. It takes a thorough knowledge of postal regulations and requirements, a considerable amount of shipping materials and insurance, and a great deal of organization.

– Do you really want to sell collectibles that might have upgrade potential in an Internet-only venue? Actually, the real question is whether or not you can recognize the pieces that have upgrade potential in the first place.

The final questions are whether you have the time and patience to accomplish this on your own, and whether the outcome is likely to be superior enough to justify your added involvement (which will be considerable). If you can answer yes to all these questions, then maybe this is not an option for you to consider and you probably don't need any further guidance from us. If not, we strongly recommend you seek a different option, as these questions just touch the surface of what can be a complex and diverse process.

TIPS FOR HEIRS: A major auction can be the best option for heirs faced with the disposition of a valuable collection, particularly if you have little or no knowledge of collectibles and are concerned about receiving fair value. In this scenario, the auctioneer is working on percentage, and your best interests and theirs are the same: the more money you make, the more money they make. Additionally, the values will be established by third parties in the competitive bidding process. The real benefit of engaging a major auction house is its versatility.

Summing up all of the methods of disposition, certain collectibles are better suited for one method, while others would benefit more from a different venue. A major company should be willing to recommend the best venue for each of your pieces and divide the collection to your best advantage. Just be sure to ask. Heritage's Trusts & Estates Department assists in just such situations and can coordinate the sale of an estate through various venues and categories of property – HA.com/estates.

1957 Fender Stratocaster, Sunburst
Sold For: $15,535 July 2010

13

Etiquette & Tips

"Tact is one of the first mental virtues, the absence of it is fatal to the best talent." – William Gilmore Simms

"Etiquette means behaving yourself a little better than is absolutely essential." – Will Cuppy

The purpose of this book is to help you plan for the future and, if you wish, to help you dispose of your collection without being taken advantage of by the government, dealers or other collectors.

It is reasonable to assume that you want to receive as much money for your collection as possible. Similarly, it is reasonable to believe that potential buyers would want to pay the least amount they can. The one thing that's absolutely certain is that everyone else will maximize their own interests. You should, too. In plain language, it is your ultimate responsibility to make your best deal at some level. Once that's understood, a combination of business and common sense, along with a little diplomacy, will usually result in an acceptable compromise.

There are certain rules of etiquette within any collectibles community. The first premise is the division of roles. If you present yourself as a dealer, you are automatically responsible for all your actions and decisions in the arena of that collectible. That means if you make a mistake, you live with it. It also imparts a certain level of responsibility toward those who are not dealers. Dealers trade with each other at wholesale levels, in part because they communicate in the same form of verbal shorthand that assumes a level of expertise. A collectible is presented, offered, inspected and purchased (or not) without fanfare, and the principals move on to the next deal.

Conversely, many collectors ask a lot of questions (and rightly so), are nervous about their acquisitions, and return a portion of those purchases after the sale. In return for this extra "maintenance," dealers charge collectors more and pay them less than they would another dealer. It is the way of the business, and perfectly justifiable, as there have to be both retail and wholesale levels for any market to function. Naturally, most collectors would like to purchase at wholesale, and occasionally, they are awarded that opportunity. Usually, the key to this is demonstrating a familiarity with wholesale market levels, negotiating pleasantly and well, and asking only pertinent questions.

The same is true on the selling side. If you give others the impression that you know what you are doing - are organized, prepared and unlikely to waste the dealer's time - you will receive the best bid or options the first time around. We recommend, however, that you do not represent yourself as a dealer. Some collectors claim to be "vest pocket" dealers in hopes of receiving higher offers. Usually, this backfires, as the dealer then feels relieved from any obligation he may have to point out to you unrecognized rarities, or other possible advantages. Be who you are, be up front, and be positive.

Any dealer bidding out your collection is being offered a valued opportunity to conduct their business. As a non-professional, you should be able to expect:

– An appointment to allow sufficient time to evaluate your collection.

– Financial and industry references at your request (and you should request them).

– Professional treatment of you and your collection with regard to both care and security.

– You should request (prior) that any items bid at $1,000 or more be identified singly, also that any article that would benefit from certification be listed.

– A written offer presented in a timely manner. The offer should be dated and any deadline noted.

– If the company has an auction house as well, and you request it, recommendations on which collectibles are better suited for auction or direct sale should also be listed.

- Prompt payment in good funds if the offer is accepted. If the collection is sold at auction, payment in good funds on the settlement date as promised.

The dealer has a right to expect certain conduct from you as well:

- That you keep any scheduled appointment and are prompt. This applies to the dealer and their staff as well.

- The collection should be as organized as possible to minimize the time necessary to evaluate and bid on it. Even a basic inventory indicating the location of each item is helpful. If the collection lends itself to grouping, this should be done beforehand. If one group out of the collection contains most of the "value," it can be presented separately.

- You should not "shop" the dealer's offer to other dealers. It's okay to tell each bidder that other bids are being sought, but you should neither reveal what the other bids are, nor the details of who is bidding. Shopping an offer for a few more dollars is strictly "bush league," and it can definitely backfire. For example, if your first bidder did not make a strong bid and you reveal the number, the second bidder may play the competition instead of the real value and you will come up short. Similarly, if you reveal the identity of those you plan to see, the bidders could collude with one another to your disadvantage. Remember, the aura of unknown competition is the strongest leverage you have to inspire dealers to figure the deal closely and make their best bids.

- You should tell the dealer "yes" or "no" in a reasonable amount of time, and that applies even if you accept another bid. It would be considerate for you to let them know the winning bid. They can learn from the experience and not feel that their time was wasted. That can be to your advantage as well, because if you bring back more collectibles for them to bid, they should both appreciate your professionalism and bid higher the next time.

Above all, you should both expect and extend courtesy. Do not waste time with a dealer who is discourteous, nor waste time responding. Ask and answer questions, but beware of becoming agitated, even if you disagree with something you hear. Your mission is to obtain the greatest possible price for your collection. To accomplish this, it is usually best to reserve judgment until all of the information has been gathered. The very person you disagreed with may be the highest overall bidder.

As stated before, the auction process is often the most compelling and beneficial option for collection disposition. A successful auction achieves the highest gross result for each lot when presented to a wide number of knowledgeable bidders, and especially when your collectibles are of choice quality. Still, there may be some items where your net result would have been better served in another venue. There is also the fact that many provisions of an auction agreement are flexible and should be negotiated.

Here are some of the issues and options:

– Ask the auctioneer's consignment coordinator to evaluate your collection and make recommendations on which articles should be auctioned and which would be better sold by another method. Ask them to explain why.

– Do you wish to be recognized for your collecting achievements? Some consignors prefer anonymity, but if you wish the recognition, becoming a signature consignor involves two factors:

• Your overall collection must be of general significant value. This could vary from auction to auction, but for a rough figure, let's use $250,000.

• Alternatively, you may have an interesting collection of a more specific focus - possibly all items are in one group or category. Don't hesitate to ask, particularly if there's a good story behind the collection!

– Auction companies charge a seller's fee and a buyer's fee to pay their expenses and earn a profit. They are motivated to receive as much for your collectibles as possible because they, in turn, will realize greater commissions. With that philosophy in mind, it becomes a matter of resources that are expended on presenting and selling lots.

If you have high-dollar, highly desirable single pieces, the auctioneer is much better off than if you have more inexpensive items, even if the total dollar value is the same. Therefore, you might be able to negotiate a lower seller's fee if you have the "right" kind of material. Other factors also apply. You should, for example, keep in mind that the lowest commission rate is not necessarily the best deal. The first consideration should be the auctioneer's capability to provide your collection with the maximum exposure and promotion. Saving an extra percentage point or two is meaningless if another auctioneer could secure an extra 20% for your collection.

    – Some people sell their collectibles unrestricted and others place a "reserve" bid to protect them from receiving what they perceive to be "too little." We believe you should place reserve bids only if you are very familiar with current markets and have good reason to believe that you will easily realize more than the reserve elsewhere if you "buy-back" the lot.

Auctioneers also have "reserve" fees, a percentage that you will pay if you do not let the item sell. These are necessary because the auctioneers must make money for their services, and a lot that does not sell is otherwise a lost opportunity. Generally, the percentage is based on the overall terms of your consignment and how realistic the auctioneer perceives your reserves to be. You should expect the reserve fee to be 5%-10%. If the amount is more than that, ask for an explanation. If the consignment coordinator says your reserve is too high, you should discuss the rationale carefully.

Consignment coordinators are usually very savvy about what works at what levels. If you don't follow their advice, you are gambling at best. Unless you're right, the auctioneer will still earn the reserve fee. You, on the other hand, will still have the article, but at a higher cost basis. Depending on the overall quality of your consignment, you may be able to negotiate better reserve terms on some or all of your collectibles.

    – Ask the consignment coordinator for the cost of photography and lotting in the auctions that you are considering. You want the maximum number of photographs and as much descriptive cataloging as possible, and this may vary depending on how much the auctioneer has to pay for the auction venue rights.

For example, in some auctions, the minimum value for a catalog photograph may be $1,500 and in others, $2,500. The latter auction, while possibly a better venue overall, might not be as beneficial for your pieces valued from $1,500 - $2,400. Similarly, each auction will have a minimum lot value. In some cases, it's $250, some $500, and in the very best of sales, it may be $1,000. Most auction companies will allow you to combine items to reach the minimum, but there is a limit to the number that may be used and still receive individual, mainstream placement. The key point for you to remember is that if your overall consignment is a good one, you may be able to negotiate a more lenient lot and photography standard.

– If you have "Large Lots" of coins, you need to determine the best arrangement to sell your coins to them profitably. Remember the rolls of "Wheat pennies" you accumulated by date and mintmark over the years? How about the five proof sets you ordered from the Mint each year for the last three decades? Or the cheaper coins that you religiously stapled into 2 by 2s and stored in 14 different stock boxes - sound familiar?

We understand that all of these purchases contributed to your collecting pleasure, but we have one question to ask: would you travel somewhere else in the country to buy them today? The answer is almost certainly, "no," and that answer applies to others as well. As discussed previously, it is the "cream" of a collection that is most likely to "over-perform" at a major auction.

Large lots are at the other end of the spectrum; it's a matter of logistics. By their very nature, large lots are bulky, cumbersome to carry to auction sites and difficult to ship once sold. They are time-consuming to catalog and require a lot of extra effort to earn the same percentage as a single coin of comparable lot value. Auction company personnel are not very fond of the large lots in major auctions and neither are most bidders, because their focus is on the more "high-powered" lots. Auctioneers will take your large lots for a big sale, but you have absolutely no leverage, and that's not what auctions are all about. In most cases, you would be better off asking the auctioneer to bid the large lots straight up. You will probably realize greater net proceeds and will be paid immediately.

Our company has an additional option, primarily for coin collectors; Heritage holds "large lot only" sales. They are not elaborate and the lots are not extensively written-up. What these auctions do attract is an enormous base of the country's strongest buyers of large lot material. These are dealers who specialize in inexpensive (relatively) coins, sets and bulk. We know who they are and they are fiercely competitive. We actually invite them to our offices three to five times annually (for the last decade) to buy the remnants of our collection purchases. They are frequently amazed at the items we have in-house for upcoming auctions. Now, we are taking consignments and letting the public in on this "well kept" secret. You do have to wait a bit longer for auction and settlement than with an outright sale, but it can be well worth it.

Occasionally, people ask us why they shouldn't dispose of their collectibles to, or through, another collector. The premise, of course, is that the collector would pay more and the playing field would be more level. There is some general merit to those statements, but there are some caveats as well:

– A collector will pay more for some items, but will rarely pay more for all of them. Take care that you don't receive a little more for the best few pieces of your collection only to find that there are no buyers for the less favorable material.

– Being a collector in and of itself is no guarantee that the individual you contact is any more or less knowledgeable or moral than a dealer. We believe that on average, dealers should be better informed on current market conditions, upgrade potential and the reputations of potential buyers. We know of at least one situation where a collector acquaintance sold a collection for heirs, only to take a bad check from the buyer. That individual was well known as a "bad egg" by the dealer community, but the collector/agent was totally unaware. It took more than a year and considerable expense for the heirs to collect a fraction of the amount owed.

– As an agent, the collector is less likely to have insurance coverage for your collection while in their care. If you use a collector, don't forget to verify this just as you would with a dealer.

The bottom line is that you should qualify a collector in the same manner as you would a dealer. While you may see some advantages in such a relationship with a collector, don't overlook dealer advantages that you may be taking for granted. Although collectors may have good intentions, a major collection should be sold only with the assistance of a qualified professional. It is unwise to rely on a part-time hobbyist to dispose of a major financial asset. In most cases you would be more successful to allow the collector bid at auction against tens of thousands of others.

The final issues of etiquette are the relationships between a collector and their heirs, and between the heirs themselves. The collector, as the owner, has all the rights and responsibilities for the collection in their lifetime, and can provide guidance (or not) to their heirs as they see fit.

That said, any guidance (as opposed to none) is often a blessing. Even if only one or a few of the heirs has any interest in the collectibles, a general understanding by all where they fit into the picture goes a long way towards familial harmony. The collector should identify and detail specific bequests if that is desirable. "Dad split them up that way in the will" is a lot more powerful than, "I'm sure Dad wanted me to have this one."

Similarly, the collector should indicate who should be contacted to help dispose of the collection - and who should not. It's amazing how many "old friends" can appear after the death of a known collector. The Executor or Trustee, whether he or she is a family member or not, should be advised of all these details.

Heirs should remember that the other heirs are also probably under a great deal of stress, so be considerate of each other. We like to think that family is the most important thing, so here are some tips to avoid controversy if the collection needs to be sold or disposed of equitably when specific guidance was not provided by the donor:

Leave the division to a third party. If the collection is not to be sold, have the appraiser separate the inventory into the appropriate number of groups by value. If one or more heirs want specific pieces, have the appraiser value those individually and if the remainder of the collection is sold, use those amounts to adjust shares accordingly. Finally, if the collection is to be disposed of, but each heir wants "something" to remember the deceased by, determine the dollar value that you want to set aside and have each heir "buy" the collectibles they want at the appraised price. In all cases, remember to keep things in perspective. The collection once provided a great deal of pleasure to your loved one, and if there is any sentiment to be attached to them, it should be a positive one.

The preparation of this handbook has been a labor of love, though by no means easy. There are two main reader groups that have been targeted by this treatise, neither of whom should be overjoyed by the implications of having to read through it. If you are a collector, the thought of estate planning may make you look closer at your own mortality. If you are an heir or possible heir of a collector, you have probably read this book because your loved one declined to face reality and left you a burden along with the inheritance.

We would take more pleasure in relating a more upbeat subject, but we will be satisfied if this handbook has made it a little easier for you to address a very difficult task.

We offer, in closing, this final guidance regardless of your circumstance or role:

1. Determine your goal.

2. Know your options.

3. Analyze them and pick the best course of action for you.

4. Make a plan.

5. If you need assistance, choose it carefully.

6. Above all, remain flexible and don't be afraid to adjust your plan as you go along.

7. Form a team of the best advisors available and pay the price now rather than later.

Good Luck!

30cm Shiny Fuchsia Porosus Crocodile Birkin
Bag with Palladium Hardware.
Sold For: $41,825 December 2010

APPENDICES

APPENDIX A

NUMISMATIC FRATERNAL ORGANIZATIONS

American Numismatic Association (ANA)
818 North Cascade Avenue
Colorado Springs, CO 80903
1-719-632-2646
FAX 1-719-634-4085
E-mail: ana@money.org
Web site: money.org

The American Numismatic Association is the country's largest collector organization for coins and related items. Formed in 1891, the ANA offers educational programs, an authentication service (no grading), and a monthly magazine, Numismatist. Its Colorado Springs headquarters features a first-rate museum and library that are available to members and non-members alike. The ANA offers renowned summer seminars on a number of numismatic subjects and holds two conventions annually. These shows offer 250 to 500 bourse tables and significant auctions. The annual convention auction (held in July or August) is frequently the highest grossing auction sale of the year.

Professional Numismatists Guild (PNG)
3950 Concordia Lane
Fallbrook, CA 92028
1-760-728-1300
FAX 1-760-728-8507
E-mail: info@pngdealers.com
Web site: pngdealers.com

The Professional Numismatists Guild is the preeminent dealer group in the coin industry. Formed in 1955 with the motto, "Knowledge, Integrity, Responsibility," the PNG accepts members only after stringent background and financial investigations, and a vote of the entire membership. Members agree to uphold a strict code of ethics and to resolve any complaints against them through binding PNG arbitration. Lists of PNG dealers are available from the organization.

American Numismatic Society (ANS)
140 William Street
New York, NY 10038
212-234-3130
FAX: 1-212-234-3381
E-mail: info@amnumsoc.org
Web site: amnumsoc.org

The American Numismatic Society was founded in 1858, and is dedicated to the serious study of numismatic items. To that end, it has an extensive research library and world-class collections, and provide members and visiting scholars with a broad selection of publications, topical meetings and symposia, fellowships and grants, honors and awards, and various educational projects. Membership information can be obtained at its Web site, or by the telephone number listed above.

APPENDIX B

INSURANCE COMPANIES OFFERING COLLECTIBLE & NUMISMATIC COVERAGE

Cleland & Associates
P O Box 899
Galveston, TX 77553-0899
1-409-766-7101
FAX: 1-409-766-7102
Contact: Richard Cleland

North American Collectibles Association
2316 Carrollton Road
Westminster, MD 21157
1-800-685-6746
1-410-857-5011
FAX 1-410-857-5259
Contact: Barbara Wingo
E-mail: nacabdw@aol.com

Woller, Seabury & Smith
1440 N. Northwest Highway
Park Ridge, IL 60068-1400
1-800-323-2106
1-847-803-3100

Hugh Wood, Inc.
(American Agent for Lloyds of London)
45 Broadway, 3rd Floor
New York, NY 10006
1-212-509-3777
FAX: 1-212-509-4906

Contact: Jack Fisher

APPENDIX C

THIRD-PARTY GRADING SERVICES

BASEBALL CARDS
Sportscard Guaranty LLC
P.O. Box 6919
Parsippany, NJ 07054-6919
1-800-SGC-9212
1-973-984-0018
FAX: 1-973-984-8447

PSA, Professional Sports Authenticator
P.O. Box 6180 Newport Beach, CA 92658
1-800-325-1121,
1-949-833-8824
FAX: 1-949-833-7955
Email: info@psacard.com
Beckett Grading Services (BGS)
beckett.com/grading

COINS
Numismatic Guaranty Corporation of America (NGC)
P.O. Box 4776
Sarasota, FL 34230
1-800-NGC-COIN toll free
941-360-3990
FAX: 941-360-2553

ANACS
P.O. Box 200300
Austin, Texas 78720-0300
1-800-888-1861
FAX: 1-512-257-5799
anacs.com

Professional Coin Grading Service (PCGS)
P O Box 9458
Newport Beach, CA 92658
1-800-447-8848
1-949-833-0600

FAX: 1-949-833-7660

COINS NEEDING CLEANING OR CONSERVATION
Numismatic Conservation Services (NCS)
P.O. Box 4750
Sarasota, FL 34230
1-866-627-2646
1-941-360-3996
ncscoin.com

COMICS
Comics Guaranty, LLC
P.O. Box 4738
Sarasota, FL 34230
1-877-NM-COMIC (toll free)
1-941-360-3991
FAX: 941-360-2558

APPENDIX D

ARTWORK & PAPER COLLECTIBLES
How to Care for Works of Art on Paper
by Francis W. Dolloff, Roy L. Perkinson
Conservation Concerns: A Guide for Collectors and Curators
by Konstanze Bachmann, Dianne Pilgrim

Caring for Your Art
by Jill Snyder, Joseph Montague, Maria Reidelbach

BASEBALL CARDS
The Official Price Guide to Baseball Cards
by James Beckett

BOOKS & MANUSCRIPTS
Antiquarian Booksellers Association of American (ABAA.org) posts links
to member published books and articles on collecting Rare Books and
Manuscripts

How to Identify and Collect American First Editions
Arco Publishing, New York (1976) – (No longer in print – ironically, you will
probably have to find a rare copy)

We also recommend:
ABEBooks.com as a source of books on the Internet

COINS
*The New York Times Guide to Coin Collecting: Do's, Don'ts, Facts, Myths,
and a Wealth of History*
by Ed Reiter

How to Grade U.S. Coins
by James L. Halperin

A Guide Book of United States Coins
by R. S. Yeoman

The Standard Catalog of World Coins
by Chester Krause & Clifford Mishler

COMICS
The Official Overstreet Comic Book Price Guide (Overstreet Comic Book Price Guide)
by Robert M. Overstreet – available digitally at HeritageComics.com

FURNITURE
The Bulfinch Anatomy of Antique Furniture:
An Illustrated Guide to Identifying Period, Detail, and Design
by Tim Forrest, Paul Atterbury

American Antique Furniture: A Book for Amateurs, Vol. 1
by Jr. Edgar G. Miller

Miller's Collecting Furniture: Facts at Your Fingertips
by Christopher Payne

GUNS
The Gun Digest Book of Modern Gun Values: For Modern Arms Made from 1900 to Present (Gun Digest Book of Modern Gun Values, 11th Ed)
by Ken Ramage

Antique Guns: The Collector's Guide
by John E. Traister

1998 Standard Catalog of Firearms: The Collector's Price & Reference Guide (8th Ed)
by Ned Schwing

JEWELRY
Signed Beauties of Costume Jewelry: Identification & Values
by Marcia Sparkles Brown

Vintage Jewelry: A Price and Identification Guide, 1920 to 1940s
by Leigh Leshner

Antique Trader Jewelry Price Guide
by Kyle Husfloen, Marion Cohen

PAINTINGS AND SCULPTURE
AskART.com
United States artists only

ArtNet.com
International artists

TOYS
Official Hake's Price Guide to Character Toys
By Ted Hake

Cartoon Toys & Collectibles Identification and Value Guide
By David Longest

ALL COLLECTIBLES AND FINE ARTS
Maloney's Antiques & Collectibles Resource Directory
By David J. Maloney, Jr.

For Additional Resources in all Collector categories, please visit our Resources list at:
HA.com, Where we will also invite you to take our Collector survey to qualify for free auction catalogs and a drawing to win valuable prizes.

1927 Lou Gehrig Game Worn New
York Yankees Jersey
Sold For: $717,000 November 2010

ABOUT THE AUTHORS

James L. Halperin

Born in Boston in 1952, Jim formed a part-time rare stamp and coin business at age 16. The same year, he received early acceptance to Harvard College. But by his third semester, Jim was enjoying the coin business more than his studies, so he took a permanent leave of absence to pursue a full-time numismatic career. In 1975, Jim supervised the protocols for the first mainframe computer system in the numismatic business, which would help catapult his firm to the top of the industry within four years. In 1982, Jim's business merged with that of his friend and former archrival Steve Ivy to form Heritage. In 1984, Jim wrote a book later re-titled "How to Grade U.S. Coins", which outlined the grading standards upon which NGC and PCGS would later be based. Jim is also a well-known futurist, an active collector of rare comic books, comic art and early 20th-century American art (view parts of his collection www.jhalpe.com), venture capital investor, philanthropist (he endows a multimillion-dollar health education foundation), and part-time novelist. His first fiction book, The Truth Machine, was published in 1996, became an international science fiction bestseller, was optioned as a feature film by Warner Brothers, and is now under development at Lions Gate. Jim's second novel, The First Immortal, was published in early 1998 and optioned as a Hallmark Hall of Fame television miniseries. All of Jim's royalties are donated to health and education charities..

Gregory J. Rohan,

At the age of eight, Greg Rohan started collecting coins and by 1971, at the age of 10, he was buying and selling coins from a dealer's table at trade shows in his hometown of Seattle. His business grew rapidly, and in 1987he joined Heritage as Executive Vice-President. Today, as a partner and as President of Heritage, his responsibilities include overseeing the firm's private client group and working with top collectors in every field in which Heritage is active. Greg has been involved with many of the rarest items and most important collections handled by the firm, including the purchase and/or sale of the Ed Trompeter Collection (the world's largest numismatic purchase according to the Guinness Book of World Records). During his career, Greg has handled more than $1 billion of rare coins, collectibles and art. He has provided expert testimony for the United States Attorneys in San Francisco, Dallas, and Philadelphia, and for the Federal Trade Commission (FTC). He has worked with collectors, consignors, and their advisors regarding significant collections of books, manuscripts, comics, currency, jewelry, vintage movie posters, sports and entertainment memorabilia, decorative arts, and fine art, to name just a few. Greg is a past Chapter Chairman for North Texas of the Young Presidents' Organization (YPO), and is an active supporter of the arts. Greg co-authored "The Collectors Estate Handbook," winner of the NLG's Robert Friedberg Award for numismatic book of the year. He previously served two terms on the seven-person Advisory Board to the Federal Reserve Bank of Dallas.

Mark Prendergast

Mark Prendergast earned his degree in Art History from Vanderbilt University and began his career in the arts working with a national dealer in private sales of 20th Century American Art. Joining Christie's in 1998 and advancing during a 10 year tenure to the position of Vice President, he was instrumental in bringing to market many important and prominent works of art, collections and estates. Based in the Heritage Houston office, he serves as Director of Trusts & Estates, providing assistance to fiduciary professionals in all aspects of appraising and liquidating their clients' tangible assets. From initial contact to final settlement, he strives to make the appraisal and auction process seamless and timely.

James L. Halperin   Gregory J. Rohan   Mark Prendergast

ABOUT THE EDITOR

Noah Fleisher is the Media and Public Relations Liaison at Heritage Auction. He received his BFA from New York University's Tisch School of the Arts in New York City and made a name for himself in the antiques and collectibles market as a writer and an editor for a variety of publications, including Antique Trader, New England Antiques Journal and Northeast Journal of Antiques and Art.

He has written several articles for digital publication Style Century Magazine, and also penned the Style Century blog, StyleWire, from May 2008 to January 2009. Noah is also the author of Warman's Antiques and Collectibles Price Guide to Mid-Century Modern Furniture, 1945-1985, now available.

ABOUT HERITAGE AUCTIONS

Heritage Auctions is the world's largest collectibles auctioneer. Our hundreds of thousands of members are a testament to our reputation for professional business practices and unprecedented knowledge in the field of collectibles. Our mission is to provide the Internet's most indispensable trading platform and source of information for serious collectors, investors, and dealers.

Heritage, established in 1976, offers a wide range of Americana, Books & Manuscripts, Fine Art, Coins, Comics & Comic Art, Currency, Entertainment Memorabilia, Jewelry & Timepieces, Movie Posters, and Sports Collectibles. We acquire the most unique items of the highest quality by searching and networking throughout the world. Our goal is to provide our customers with the largest selection of high-quality collectibles. We give our customers unprecedented access to our services using the latest advancements in technology and by maintaining a strong presence in the collectibles community. Our knowledgeable staff and our suite of services help our customers develop the best collections possible.

We are always looking to acquire interesting items, whether through consignment or by outright purchase, and we spend millions each month to keep our clients' demands satisfied. Find out why you should consign to a Heritage Auction at HA.com.

Heritage Trusts & Estates Services

Individuals and collectors, as well as trustees, executors and fiduciaries responsible for estate tangible property, can avail themselves of the best suite of estate services anywhere, including authoritative estate appraisals, estate planning assistance, auction services and private treaty sales.

Inquiries:
Mark Prendergast
Director of Trust & Estates
214-409-1632
Or 800-872-6467 ext. 1632
MPrendergast@HA.com

Heritage Auctions Appraisal Services

Heritage offers the highest caliber of experts to evaluate and appraise your art and collectibles. Working with our appraisal team, you will receive thorough, illustrated appraisal reports written in compliance with all IRS, USPAP and Insurance standards. At competitive rates, a Heritage appraisal should be considered for all Estate Tax ,Charitable Donation, Insurance, Estate or Financial Planning situations.

Inquiries:
Meredith Meuwly
Director of Appraisal Services
214-409-1631
Or 800-872-6467 ext. 1631
MeredithM@HA.com